NATURAL BIRDHOUSES

NATURAL BIRDHOUSES

AMEN & MARIA FISHER

APPLE

Contents

Project Selector

Introduction

The natural birdhouses in this book have been designed by two nature lovers with a soft spot for birds. Our unique line of birdhouses, called Given Back Bird Houses, encompasses a huge variety of songbird houses, feeders, open nesters, bat houses, pollinator houses, tree stands and nurse logs. This book represents our finest work.

In the true spirit of pioneering naturalists, we disregarded all modern bird charts, which are based on milled timber and squares, and went back to science and history for the basis of our designs. Together, we did exhaustive research from the life works of several historical ornithologists, and subsequently created a whole line of exact replicas of wild bird habitats.

Our products are all 100 per cent original designs, perfected by us over the years. Built to last for generations, these birdhouses are so carefully constructed that they can withstand the most extreme weather.

We also developed our own hanging system, in which the wire runs all the way around the house, cradling the entire weight from underneath. The wire is formed into a releasable loop on top, which allows the house to hang from any branch easily, safely and without disturbing the tree.

We start by collecting deadwood and driftwood pieces, as well as different types of mosses, cones, fallen bark and branches.

We hollow out each piece of wood to the dimensions needed to best fit tiny songbirds, like the various nuthatches, chickadees and wrens. We have come up with an open nester design that invites such birds as robins, finches and hummingbirds to take advantage of the camouflage that these shelters provide. Pollinator houses are tiny replicas of our birdhouses, fitted with specific holes to give pollinating insects like moths, bees and butterflies their own little habitats too. We have also developed specific bluebird housing, bat habitats and much-needed owl houses, to answer the call of these other cavity nesters in the wild.

Before the houses are ready, we attach the materials we have collected to attract the birds and to provide them with supplies for their nest inside. While not unbalancing any one ecosystem, we carefully take only what we need to create these one-of-a-kind bird, bug and bat habitats. Finally, these little houses are hung in the garden, and the wood is truly given back to the birds.

Since we first began Given Back Bird Houses in 2009, people have been asking how we make them. And now, with this book, we are sharing our coveted building and decorating techniques for the first time in print.

Happy home building!

Amen & Maria Fisher
www.GivenBackBirdHouses.com

GETTING STARTED

Attracting Wildlife to Your Garden

Creating a healthy ecosystem in your own garden is both satisfying and rewarding. The simple act of placing habitats, food and water in your garden is the start of attracting a full ecosystem. By consciously setting out these necessities, you have a chance to positively interact with nature.

Bird habitats

Putting up enough bird habitats to support a varied population is incredibly rewarding. Witnessing successful nesting is a miracle that never gets worn out. Wild birds add a whole rhythm to the day. They begin the morning with cheerful wake-up songs, they chatter all day about their goings-on, they have alarm calls when a predator enters the landscape and, perhaps most satisfying, they sing the day to a close with their own evening rituals and songs.

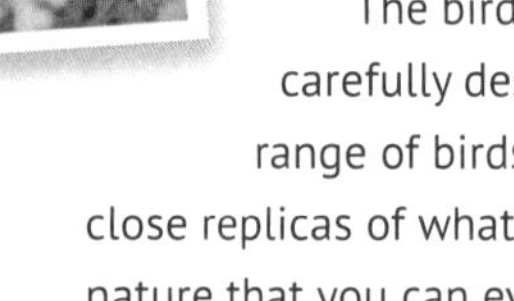

The birdhouses in this book are carefully designed to attract a wide range of birds. In fact, they are such close replicas of what wild birds would find in nature that you can even attract choosy ones.

Feeding your birds

Wild birds need drinking water year-round. In a time of drought, a dish of water is a necessity. Even in the snow, it provides welcome respite. Fill water dishes every day for all of your wild friends. Plus, you will enjoy watching the drinking habits of each visitor.

By building and using our feeders, you are providing a food source, which is the most appealing attractor. Second, you are inviting the shy birds to come out of the bushes and off the ground so that you may enjoy them. You get to witness them up close, watch their varied and frequently comical eating habits and see how different birds fly. By providing seed and suet, you are also ensuring that when they do eat an insect, it is the one right next to them in your garden. Birds are happy to share pest control, your toughest gardening task.

Bees also need the fluff that birds use for nesting as something to burrow down into.

Pollinators

Another creature that often depends on deadwood is the mason bee, which seeks out the same sapless deadwood as the birds do for nesting. The mason bee is not aggressive by nature. By packing walls of pollen between its eggs, this bee is an important little pollinator. It has a high tolerance for cool temperatures and so works a long season, pollinating twenty times more than any other creature.

Bumblebees are another favourite pollinator. In the early cold spring, they often look for holes in deadwood to go nestle in the fluff left over by last year's nesters. Giving them a house of their own ensures that your garden will have a stable population of these non-aggressive pollinators. We use a hole sized just for them, so that they do not have to compete for housing.

Planting for wildlife

Growing flowers and herbs that attract pollinators is also important to the ecosystem you are creating. Without those vital plants, they have no food, and then would not be able to procreate, even with the correct habitats hanging. The pollinators' presence is self-perpetuating – their behaviour naturally makes more flowers, and with more flowers they can eat more and make more babies.

Our Nurse Log Planter (page 116) is a perfect vessel for growing flowers. Bumblebees use their legs to comb through each part of the flower thoroughly, collecting pollen as they go.

Night creatures

Making bat habitats is the perfect way to ensure that bats come around at night. Most microbats eat insects, and some are avid night pollinators as well. Not only can each bat eat a thousand insects every night, but their excrement, guano, is one of the best fertilisers recognised by gardeners worldwide. While many people put up bat houses for insect control, many others collect the prized fertiliser from underneath and mix it in with their garden soil. Microbats use echolocation to navigate. This makes them all the more fascinating to watch as they perform their acrobatics in your garden at dusk.

Along with bats at night, you might hope to host an owl or two on your property as well. A healthy owl population signals a healthy ecosystem, and these birds also provide a good form of effortless and humane rodent control.

Choosing and Collecting Wood

Birds in the wild consider deadwood the perfect nesting material. Deadwood is any tree that has stood in the forest, then died of old age or other natural causes and drained off its sap as it dried. The best wood is porous and swaddled in bark.

Deadwood

Deadwood may stand in the forest for decades, housing generations of cavity nesters, but much of it is naturally blown down each year by strong winds and storms. Then you can collect it freely from the forest floor with the permission of the forest owner, or according to your local forest regulations.

As far as type of wood goes, nothing is as important as the fact that it has to be deadwood. Whether your wood is hard like apple, oak and hemlock; medium like Douglas fir, maple and redwood; or soft like cedar, birch, pine and alder, it can be successfully used. The most important characteristic is that it is void of tree sap. Without sap, mould and bacteria, which would be harmful to newborn baby birds, are unable to grow.

The first thing to do when you go into the forest to seek out downed trees is to try to get to a high elevation. This gives you a view of the forest floor, allowing your eyes to find the horizontal lines of downed trees. Once you spot a tree, you can hike over to it. Look for sections of wood that are 6–10in (15–25cm) in diameter and then test for suitability.

Bad deadwood: too rotten

Too green, wood splitting

Good deadwood: has a natural break, is not fully on the ground

Mushrooms grow on deadwood: easy to spot!

Testing for suitability

First, check for visible rot, such as large chunks of missing bark. If you do not see any, get a little closer to look for holes that indicate the wood has already been hollowed out by insects. If you find a section without insect holes, put your hands around the log and feel for soft spots up and down. Sometimes a log will look pristine and intact, but when you squeeze around it, your fingers can poke right through the bark, signalling rot. If it feels uniformly firm and dry, proceed to the next step.

This is what we call 'listening to the wood'. The best way to do this is to knock on the log with a solid stick. Listen for a sound that resonates, which is an indicator of dry wood. If the log is wet, it will make a thick, thudding noise.

If the log sounds dry, make a single cut, using a hand or petrol-powered saw, depending on the forest regulations. Look at the wood inside to check for signs of moisture penetration, such as dark spots or a dark wet ring around the inside of the bark. Also look for evidence of damage by insects.

Great deadwood will be firm inside, dry to the touch and will not feel sticky at all. At this point, cut the log into sections you can comfortably carry. Luckily, deadwood only weighs about a third as much as a green log.

Driftwood

The same rules apply when finding driftwood or drifted logs along beaches or river edges. About 90 per cent of the driftwood we come across is not suitable for birdhouses. Look for signs of whether the tree was alive or dead when it came down. You can tell that a wood had been green because it develops big splits, and the bark is popping off and sometimes is still hanging onto green leaves or needles. Chainsaw cuts usually indicate a tree was alive when it came down. Don't be fooled: just because a piece of wood looks old, with a silver patina, it may not be suitable birdhouse wood. All the same checks need to be made on driftwood logs, regardless of outer appearance.

Local knowledge

In urban and suburban areas, a great way to find birdhouse wood is to talk to your local firewood supplier or the tree care expert in your area. Both are experts in wood, know how to recognise deadwood and often have large sections available to sell or share.

Also ask the elder woodworkers in your area for tips about local wood safety. Our area grows Port Orford cedar, for example, which can cause kidney and liver damage if you breathe its sawdust. In fact, we are always careful with cedar sawdust of any type for this same reason; it can cause 'cedar fever', which feels like a fever and sinus infection together. Most of the trees you will find in your garden are safe, but it is worth knowing this localised information.

Tip: Never cut down standing deadwood, which is vital to the survival of too many species to list. Use only what has already been blown to the ground.

Basic Techniques

All of the projects in this book follow the same step-by-step procedure: marking the design onto the log; cutting out all the pieces; joining the components together; and finally adding a hanging system. No specialist woodworking machinery is required, and the basic techniques involved are easy to master.

MARKING THE LOG

Always look straight down on the log from above when marking, as this will make it easier to mark a straight line on a curved surface. Because of the irregularity of raw timber, it is preferable to use the centre line of the log as a baseline for all measurements (rather than measuring from one end or the other). Always brush off the log before beginning to mark it.

1 A carpenter's pencil works well on light-coloured surfaces because it sands off easily afterwards. On a barked log, try a timber-marking crayon or coloured pencil to show against the dark ridges. Make sure the marks are thick and clear enough to be visible.

2 Later, if you feel comfortable with the technique, try a scribe or saw blade, which clearly marks any wood surface.

It is very important to mark the cut lines only in the order the project states. This will save you time in the long run. After you cut, clearly mark the end grain of each piece with an arrow pointing in the direction of the front of the birdhouse, to ease the reassembly process.

TOOLS AND SUPPLIES

The following list includes the tools and materials commonly used to make the projects in this book.

Cutting

- Reciprocating saw with wood/metal plunging blades: 6in (150mm), 9in (230mm), 12in (300mm)
- Chainsaw with 16in (400mm) blade (optional)

NOTE:
For projects that require a diameter of wood that is 5in (12.5cm) or less, choose the 6in (150mm) blade; for a 5–8in (12.5–20cm) diameter piece of wood, use the 9in (230mm) blade; and for diameters 9in (23cm) and above, use the 12in (300mm) blade.

Drilling

- Hand drill
- **Paddle bits** in sizes: ¾in (18mm), 1⅛in (29mm), 1¼in (32mm), 1½in (38mm)
- **Regular drill bits** in sizes: ¼in (6mm) diameter by 8–12in (20–30cm) length, and ½in (12mm) by 12in (30cm) length
- **Regular drill bits** in sizes: ⅛in (3mm), 3/16in (5mm), ¼in (6mm), ⅜in (9mm), ½in (12mm)

Chiselling

- ½in (12mm) chisel and dead-blow mallet

Joining

- Nail gun with capacity to shoot 2in (50mm) nails

Sanding

- Sanding disc drill attachment with 60-grit stick-on sandpaper

General tools

- Needle-nose pliers
- Pin hammer
- Cross-head screwdriver
- Wood rasp in half round/half flat
- Wire snippers
- Garden secateurs

Supplies

- Finish nails (such as panel pins or fine-gauge lost-head nails) in sizes: 1in (25mm), 1½in (40mm), 1¾in (45mm), 2in (50mm)
- Exterior screws (such as deck screws): 2in (50mm), 3in (75mm)
- 2in (50mm) ring nails
- Exterior waterproof wood glue with 1in (2.5cm) glue brush
- PVC-coated 16-gauge tie wire
- Uncoated 16-gauge tie wire
- 120-grit sandpaper sheets
- Pure beeswax and tung oil mix (page 22)
- Rag for buffing
- Bristle brush

SAFETY GEAR

- Clear safety glasses or goggles
- Dust mask
- Protective trousers for your legs while using chainsaw
- Ear defenders or earplugs
- Gloves (you will need dexterity, so mechanic's gloves are our favourite)

It can be easy to dismiss safety gear as 'extra' or unnecessary, but it is vital to your work. Preventing accidents or injuries is the most important part of being able to move on to the next project. Please consider making substitutions to the tools and supplies list if you have to, rather than omitting or altering any of this safety gear. We use every item, every time.

Important rule about gloves: Never wear gloves when using any drill. Always use bare hands, and keep all material, straps and long hair away from the spinning mechanism.

CUTTING THE LOG

Strapping and clamping

Secure each piece of wood tightly and carefully before you begin using power tools. This will help you make cleaner cuts and also minimise the risk of injury. A canvas strap works well, as shown here, as does a bar or sash clamp. Always work on a flat surface. Test to make sure the wood does not move around and cannot be easily dislodged before you begin.

Cutting with a reciprocating saw

It is important to use the length of saw blade called for in each project. Always place the blade firmly on the wood before pulling the trigger. Do not start the blade motion in the air.

1 To cut a log into sections, place the saw blade on the surface of the log, then pull the trigger and saw back and forth in a rocking motion (think of using a hand saw in a see-saw motion). You want a clean, straight cut without marking the bark, which is particularly important for roof and floor cuts (try to avoid touching the bark with the blade guard). Watch both sides of the saw blade carefully to make sure you are following the marked lines.

2 When plunging into a drill hole when hollowing out a log, put the saw blade tip into the hole and then pull the trigger gently until the blade catches. You can finesse it and let the blade pull itself through to the other side. Once the blade is through, use the guard against the wood and keep the blade angled towards the next drill hole. Once you feel the blade go into the next drill hole, stop sawing, pull the blade out and begin this technique anew, on the angle to the next drill hole.

Cutting with a chainsaw

Never attempt to use a chainsaw before being instructed on how to handle it, and always read all safety material that accompanies your purchase. All our projects can be done without a chainsaw, if you would prefer. However, if you would like to use one, please do not even switch it on until you have put on all your safety gear, including eye, ear and leg protection.

1 When cutting wood with a chainsaw, it is vital to be aware that there is always the possibility of kickback. This occurs when the tip of the blade touches a surface head on, bounces off and comes back at you. Bearing that in mind, position your body in such a way that the blade cannot hit you. Keep your body perpendicular to the blade and away from the arc of cutting. Always keep your toes and face in mind so that the chainsaw will never have a chance to injure you.

2 To plunge through wood when hollowing out, set the blade running and get a little groove started that is about 1½in (4cm) deep, perpendicular to the log end grain. Gently rock back and forth and you will feel the blade move forwards about ½in (12mm) each time. Once the blade tip peeks through the other side, slow your motion just a little bit and let the blade work through the last part itself. Once the whole blade is through the log, very carefully follow your marked cut line in both directions and then stop. Repeat this three more times to cut the shape of a square, which then lets you remove the middle in one piece. Always keep looking down and checking that you are following the marked lines.

HOLLOWING METHODS

The cutting techniques on pages 18–20 can be combined in several ways to hollow out a log to create the cavity of your birdhouse. In this book, we show you five ways, to accommodate the hard and soft deadwoods of your region. Although each project recommends a method, you can vary this depending on the wood you have found and the technique you prefer. Methods 1, 3 and 4 use a reciprocating saw for cutting.

1: Drill-cut-chisel, Project 1 (page 32)
2: Drill-chisel, Project 2 (page 38)
3: Cut-cut-chisel, Project 4 (page 46)
4: Cuts only, Project 6 (page 52)
5: Drill only, Project 17 (page 98)

Drilling

Always drill away from all body parts. Start with the tip of the drill bit positioned on the wood before you pull the trigger. Once the bit is in the wood, keep it on the same trajectory in a straight line.

1 Regular drill bit: Always drill in and out, over and over, back and forth, until you come out the other side. Never force the bit through or it just snaps inside the wood.

2 Paddle bit: A paddle bit does not automatically pull the wood shavings out of the hole, so you have to help it along by backing it out a little bit at a time to let the wood chips come out. Once you feel the paddle tip begin to exit out of the other side, ease off the tension and let the blade do the work. This will keep it from blowing out the other side.

3 Auger (boring) bit: Make sure that you line up the bit accurately before you pull the trigger. This is a fast and unforgiving bit that pulls itself through the wood. Auger bits are generally designed to pull the wood shavings out as you go. However, once you have drilled about halfway through, pull it back a little in case sawdust is building up in the hole.

Chiselling

The purpose of chiselling is to follow the wood's natural curvature to create a round cavity. Chiselling is often easier and always safer than machining an irregular log. Stand the wood on its end grain on a flat surface and use a dead-blow mallet to strike the chisel; it has a wide base and good shock absorption. Make sure that you always chisel away from yourself and all body parts, chiselling towards the centre of the log to create a round shape inside.

JOINING THE PIECES

Gluing

Gluing wood together is so strong that it outranks nailing. The combination of the two that we use creates the strongest possible permanent bond. Before applying any glue, brush off both pieces of wood well and fit them together, using your alignment arrows (page 16) and matching up the woodgrain or bark grooves. When you are happy with the positioning of the pieces, apply glue to both surfaces, press them together snugly and then nail in a crisscrossing pattern (see panel, right). When gluing to seal wood (page 23), cover the end grain with a layer of glue that is thick enough to penetrate. Always let glue dry thoroughly; overnight is ideal. Always use water-based glue, so it will not harm the birds.

Tip: Put a handful of wood chips or shavings into the cavity of the birdhouse before gluing on the roof. This gives the birds something to excavate.

Nailing

When nailing two pieces of wood together, never put a nail in straight. Always angle nails in alternating directions, creating a crisscross pattern. This anchors the pieces and prevents the nails from being pulled out. We use finish nails (the type used for attaching beading and moulding, such as panel pins) because they are much thinner in gauge than construction nails and have a small nail head that almost disappears into the wood. Use galvanised or stainless steel to avoid rusting on these long-lasting outdoor projects.

JOINING A BASE

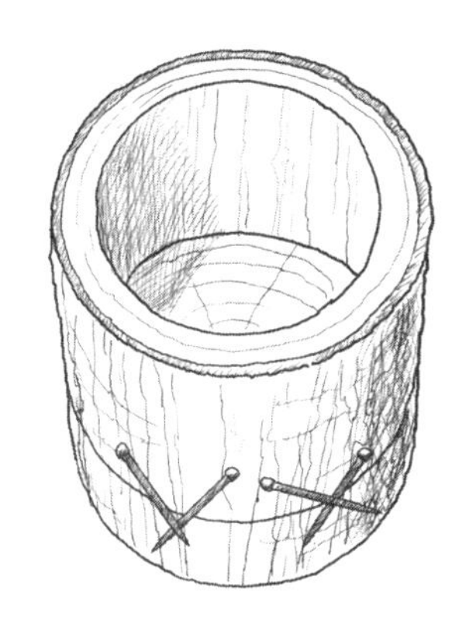

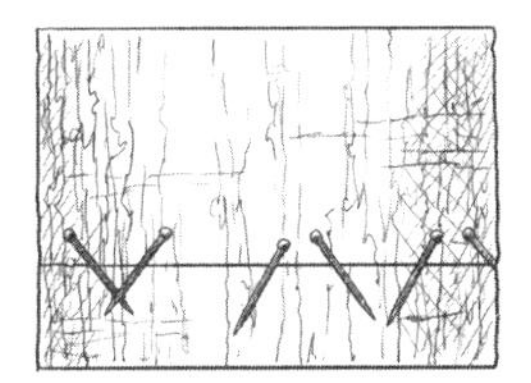

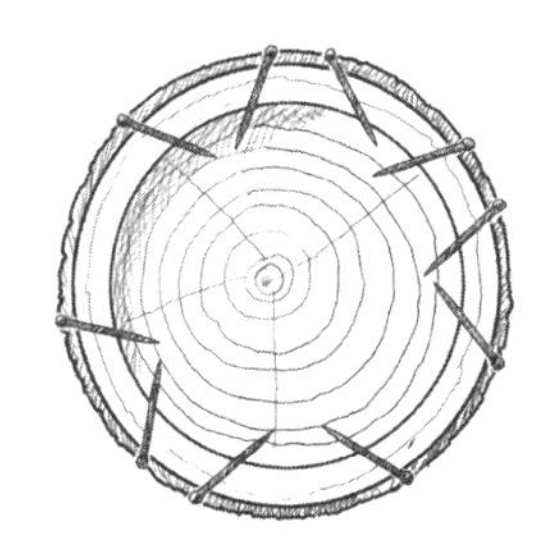

JOINING ROOFS AND SIDES

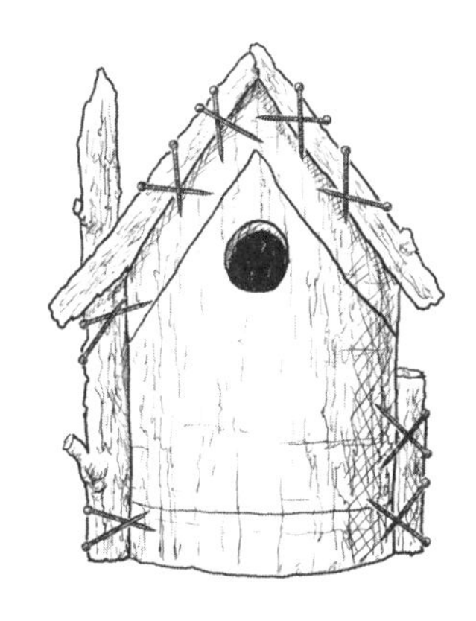

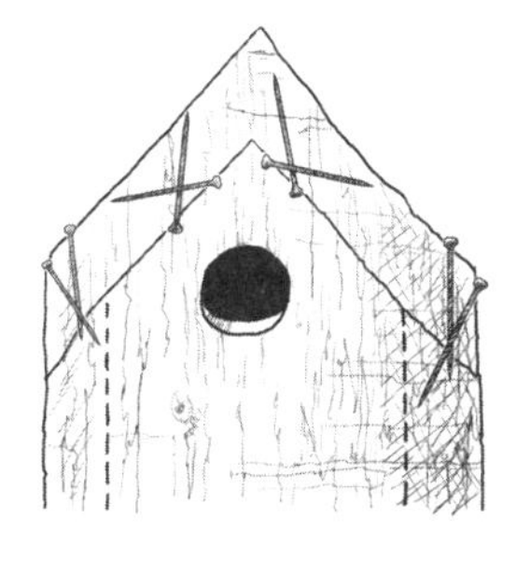

ADDING DECORATIONS

FINISHING

Sanding

Sanding wood brings out the lustre of the woodgrain. Start with a coarse-grade sandpaper, like 60- or 80-grit, using a circular motion. You may use a powered sander or do it by hand. We use a drill attachment combined with hand finishing to create our look. The first goal is to flatten the biggest grooves. Then step down to around 120-grit sandpaper and sand with the grain. Work until you get the look you want; a rough surface gives a rustic look, and a very smooth surface looks elegant and refined.

Always wear a dust mask when sanding, especially with cedar woods. A breathing mask is also good when cutting outdoors, where wind kicks up sawdust.

Waxing

Tung oil is a natural product drawn from the nuts of the tung tree that, when mixed with beeswax, produces a long-lasting, non-toxic wood finish that seals, beautifies, protects and waterproofs raw sanded wood surfaces.

1 You will need 1 cup of 100 per cent pure beeswax, melted, and 1 cup of tung oil. Mix the melted wax and oil together thoroughly and pour into a glass jar. When cool, cover with a lid and use as needed.

2 To apply the wax and oil treatment, warm it in your hands first to make it malleable. Then rub it into the sanded wood surfaces by hand until you see the wood soak it up. Once the surface is covered with hand-warmed wax, let it cool for about 10 minutes to harden. Then buff briskly with a soft cloth. Repeat the process one or two more times. Water will bead up on the surface now.

Sanded wood

Waxed wood

Making hanging wire

Cut double the appropriate length of wire for the project you are working on. This means it should go roughly all the way around the house, plus 2ft (60cm) more. Put both ends into an empty drill. Put the loop on a nail or other firm holder and pull taut. Start the twist and continue until it is twisted enough to pull the drill about an inch closer to the loop end. Then release the drill and use wire cutters to cut both ends clean.

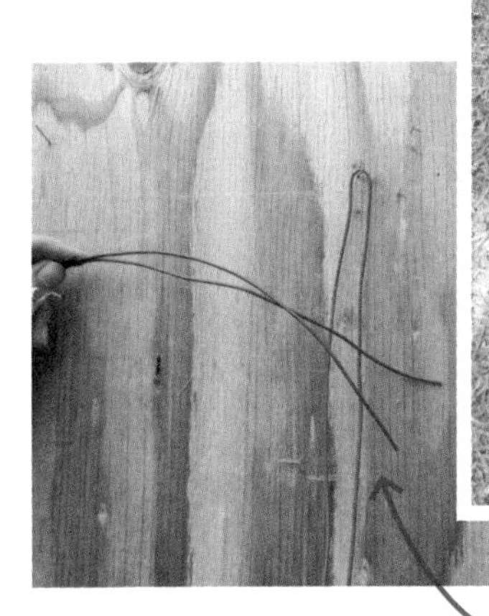

We generally use 16-gauge PVC-coated tie wire, doubled, to hang our houses.

Releasable loop

Insert the hanging wire through the drill holes you made in your birdhouse during the step-by-step instructions. The wire should extend about 18in (45cm) above the peak of the roof on one side and about 6in (15cm) above on the other. Meet both wire ends at the peak and twist them together until you have about 2in (5cm) directly above the house. Now curl the short loop into a swirl and the long one into a bigger swirl. These can be linked onto each other to form a releasable loop.

SEALING THE END GRAIN

Applying glue (page 21) to all of the end grain on the finished birdhouse will completely seal the wood in a non-toxic way. We usually seal the wood after assembling the hanging wire system and then leave the birdhouse hanging overnight to dry before applying decorations to the house. Sometimes we wax the face of the house before gluing the end grain to protect the sanded surface from the glue.

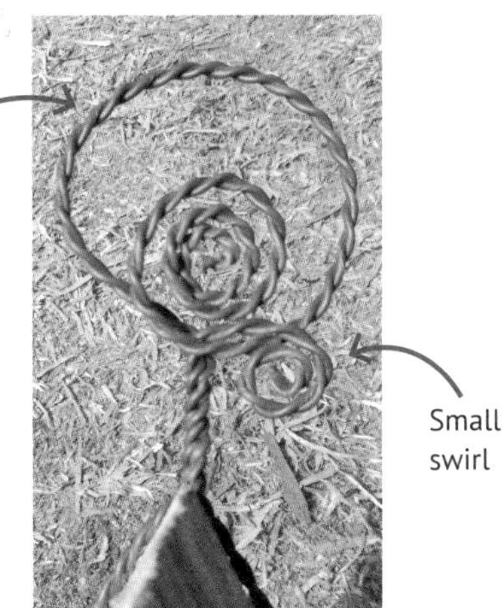

Decorating Your Houses

Decorations take our log houses from rough wood to beautiful artwork. Sticks create perches and shingles protect the roof underneath while adding character and style. Mosses, lichens and cones add colour contrast, textural elements and sometimes the illusion of landscaping in miniature.

Collecting materials

All collecting can be done without disturbing or stripping the natural areas you collect from. To do this, take only small amounts of each thing at a time. Take just a handful of cones, for example, from under each tree, so that there are still enough left for the squirrels.

When collecting moss, take only about 8in (20cm) diameter from every 4ft (1.2m) radius of a mossy forest floor. Then fill the bald section in a bit with the moss from around the edges of this gap. This technique helps mosses regrow easily.

Try to go to different locations each time, and avoid collecting from spots visible from the trails. This ensures undisturbed beauty for everyone enjoying the forest.

Types of decoration

Use strong sticks and pinecones to decorate these houses and feeders. They are made to be hanging for decades, so the quality of what you apply to the outside needs to be topnotch. With your hands, try to break sticks that are under 12in (30cm) long. Anything you cannot easily break is durable enough to use as decorations. Use the toughest sticks and fruitwood branches, and look for sticks with interesting shapes. Turning and twisting can be very visually appealing.

Conifer cones make great decorations. Pinecones can be really good and tough, especially beach pines. Spruce cones are beautiful and deceptively durable. Fir cones are wonderful when fresh.

Bark also makes great decorations. Bark pieces that are ½–1in (12–25mm) thick are best for roof shingles. Alternatively, you can make shingles from the centre block of the birdhouse that is removed when you hollow out the log. Stand the block up on end on a stump, as you would for chopping firewood. Using a sharp axe, split off pieces as thinly as possible.

Cut your own shingles.

Your goal is ¼in (6mm) thick shingles in whatever shape the block is in.

Moss is a great way to decorate houses in wet or shady areas. Mosses are antibacterial and help to purify the air inside the wooden cavity. Birds will take moss off the outside of the house and use it inside the nest. Moss can be found on the backs of trees and along the tops of branches. Finding water sources often helps you locate mosses and lichens.

Tip: You can use any found materials from the woods and hedgerows to decorate your finished birdhouses: bark, moss and twigs are all bird friendly.

Attaching decorations

Use at least three nails for every single piece to be attached. Insert all nails in a crisscross fashion (page 21). Nails must be long enough to penetrate the main body of the birdhouse, so that the decoration is held securely in place, but not so long that they pierce the cavity and create a pincushion effect inside.

Whenever possible, attach items to the solid roof and floor of the birdhouse rather than the hollow midsection. Attaching multiple sticks to these parts of the house also serves to strengthen its overall structural integrity. Everything should be so securely attached that you can hold the weight of the house by each individual piece. Test this by picking up the house by its roof shingles, then pick it up by each stick you have attached.

The best way to attach moss is to nail it down, roots and all, with the solid pieces that you are using to decorate the house. First lay the moss on the main body of the house, then place sticks and cones strategically to hold the moss in place. This technique allows the moss to regrow each season and to get enough water to its viable roots. You can attach lichens in the same way.

Mounting and Positioning

It is important to position your birdhouses and feeders in locations that will provide the birds with shelter and protection. Never put birdhouses or feeders on the ground because this leaves your birds vulnerable to attack by cats, rats and other predators.

Songbird houses

When hanging a birdhouse in a tree, the house should be about 6ft (1.8m) up and 2ft (60cm) out from the trunk. Cats prefer to rob nests that are close to the tree trunk. Use the releasable hanging loop (page 23) to wrap around a branch and then hook back onto itself. If using a hook, wrap the loop around the hook an extra time to make a secure connection.

When mounting a house, the bottom of the house is solid timber. You can place the house on a flat wood surface like a cut-off tree or a wooden post. Pre-drill through both the stand and the house, and then attach with three or four 3in (75mm) deck screws. Alternatively, make a Tree Stand (page 86).

Always put birdhouses 30ft (9m) away from birdfeeders. This distance gives bird parents a comfortable buffer from visiting eaters. For the same reason, do not hang the house above a spring or summer berry patch. If you have made a fluff dispenser, hang it about 6ft (1.8m) off the ground. Birds need to be able to concentrate on collecting without being ambushed by a cat.

Do not position your birdhouse where the prevailing wind blows directly into the entrance hole.

Owl and woodpecker houses

These two birds want to nest as high as possible. In the forest, this can be in a tree anywhere from 50ft (15m) up all the way down to 10ft (3m) off the ground. Owls prefer to have a nest with a view of a meadow or a down-sloping landscape. You could even put an owl house on the roof peak of your house, garage or shed. You could raise a large 4x4in (10x10cm) post in your garden and mount your owl house on that with four 3in (75mm) deck screws.

With high timber around, use an extension ladder and then mount the house on a shelf with brackets, or use a strong branch/hook to hang it. Owls typically want to see the same house for two years before deeming it safe enough to inhabit, but will then come back to the same house every year.

Open nesters

Open nesters can function as roosts for birds overnighting in your garden, providing both shelter and camouflage. The moss bed inside also provides a measure of warmth and comfort.

Small open nesters for hummingbirds have specific instructions. Due to their long beaks, hummingbirds cannot roll their own eggs the way that other birds can. They need their nest in a place that gets a lot of movement by the wind.

Large open nesters accommodate robins, for example. Robins often want a tree trunk or wall at their back and a 180-degree view of their surroundings, preferably with heavy foliage overhead. Areas under your eaves can mimic those conditions. A large open nester placed in the trees would also be appealing to a thrush or a towhee.

Place any size open nester under your eaves to invite birds to live among your hanging flower baskets. These potential residents include finches, sparrows, robins and hummingbirds.

Pollinator houses

We have seen mason bees packing chambers that are fully exposed to sun and wind as well as in shady forest nooks, so simply hang your pollinator houses wherever you can see them. In your flowerbeds on shepherd hooks, in branches near your windows, in orchards or along a path or driveway are all good choices.

Bumblebees like to be in the sunlight starting in the early morning, if possible. They like the warmth and will gravitate towards the bushes that get the most warm light. Place their habitats close to or in flowering shrubs.

Bat houses

Mount bat houses on a tall 4x4in (10x10cm) post, the side of your house or a tree, 15–20ft (4.5–6m) up. Mount in a place with southern-facing exposure. Bats depend on daytime warmth from the sun while they are sleeping.

If you have noticed bats living in your loft or eaves, seal it up in winter while they are gone and place a bat habitat as close as possible before they return in the spring. They will gladly use the bat house instead. If the location is not ideal for you, by the second spring you can move the house somewhere more convenient and the same bats should find it again.

There are two bat houses in this book, with a double or a single chamber.

Birdhouse Sizes

Strangely enough, our whole business is based on ignoring modern bird charts. Those charts are based on squares and milled timber, not on science. The bird habitats that we make are exact replicas of recorded wild bird cavities. As a result, our size guidelines feature different categories and dimensions than a standard chart copied from the computer.

SMALL SONGBIRD

Log diameter:

5–8in (12–20cm)

Typical house size inside:

3–5in (7–12cm) in diameter, 4–7in (10–18cm) deep

Entrance hole:

1⅛–1¼in (29–32mm)

Suited to wrens, chickadees, titmice, nuthatches, small woodpeckers, sparrows and many other small size songbirds. We have heard that even some small birds that will not use square boxes do want and will use our wild bird cavities!

LARGE SONGBIRD

Log diameter:

9–15in (23–38cm)

Typical house size inside:

Less than 4in (10cm) in diameter, 7–10in (18–25cm) deep

Entrance hole:

1½in (38mm) upwards

Birds including medium-sized woodpeckers, starlings and many other songbirds will make their home in these boxes.

SMALL OWLS AND KESTRELS

Log diameter:

15in (38cm) or bigger

Typical house size inside:

Less than 8in (20cm) in diameter, 10–14in (25–36cm) deep

Entrance hole:

3in (75mm) upwards

A house size that is perfect for many larger birds, these boxes will attract small owls, kestrels and large woodpeckers – maybe even squirrels.

Clean-outs

Our houses for songbirds do not have a clean-out (an access point designed for cleaning out the cavity) because the birds do their own housekeeping, working fastidiously in the spring to prepare their nests and show off their skills to the opposite sex. These houses are cleanable, however. Look inside the cavity with a dental mirror and a torch. If you want to clean it out, turn the house upside down and give it a shake. Poke the drain hole clear with a wire, and then insert the wire through the entrance hole to hook and pull out the nest. Alternatively, clear the drain hole and then use a vacuum to suck out the nest. You can even fill the birdhouse with water, shake and then use a wet and dry vacuum.

If you are determined to include a clean-out, there are four ways demonstrated in this book that can be easily translated to the songbird houses. Those are Projects 9, 13, 21 and 22 (pages 66, 80, 108 and 112).

A little door on the back of the Owl House (Project 13, page 80) opens up to allow you to clean out the cavity.

BATS

Log diameter:

15in (38cm) cut in half, or similarly sized driftwood

Our design is based on a dead tree that has fractured inside and is listing slightly to one side – the perfect home for microbats. In nature, grooves occur from the separation of the woodgrain; a groove roughly ¾in (18mm) that runs vertically and at a slight angle is ideal. Our bat houses accommodate many species of these picky little night flyers.

POLLINATORS

Log diameter:

3–5in (7–12cm)

Chamber (drill hole) size:

3⁄16–3⁄8in (5–9mm)

These houses are designed for all kinds of pollinating insects. Based on the holes made in deadwood branches by beetles, carpenter bees or left behind by woodpeckers, these houses have chambers designed for mason bees of varying sizes and will also attract ladybirds, some butterflies and many other little insects looking for a home. You may even get pollinating moths looking for a safe place to make a cocoon.

BUMBLEBEES

Log diameter:

4–5in (10–12cm)

Typical house size inside:

3in (7.5cm) in diameter, 4in (10cm) deep

Entrance hole:

¾in (18mm)

Bumblebees buzz around birdhouses looking for the warm and dry conditions found inside natural deadwood cavities, especially when they are positioned in the sun. We have designed the pollinators so that these precious creatures do not have to compete for housing.

THE PROJECTS

Flat-top Birdhouse

This is the first wild bird habitat that we designed. It is an exact replica of a pygmy nuthatch house found in a dead standing tree. With its flat top, this is the easiest type of house that you can make with a log, and so it's a great project to get used to working with wood in the round.

CUTTING GUIDE

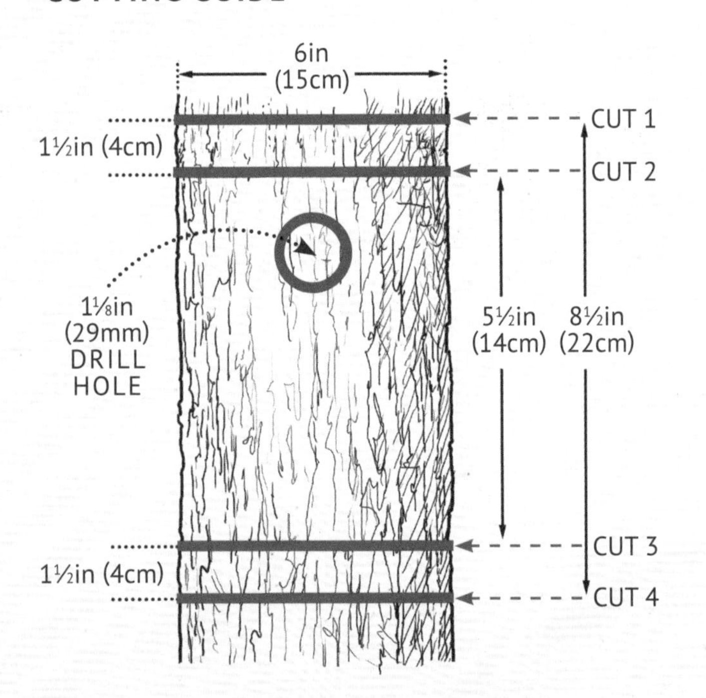

KEY

CUT LINES

HOUSE COMPONENTS

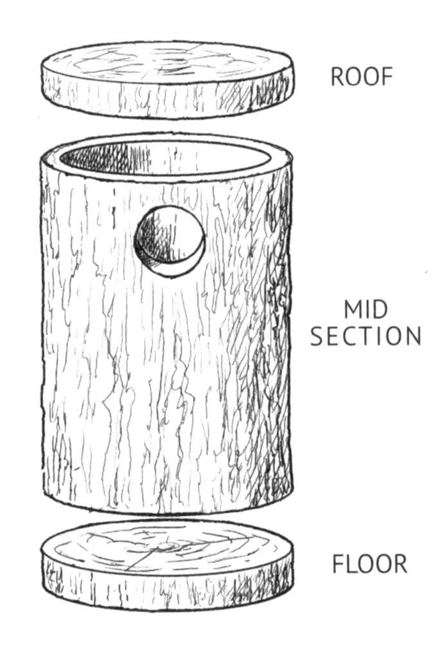

CUTTING THE LOG

1 Find a deadwood log 5–6in (12.5–15cm) in diameter and 12–18in (30–46cm) long. Brush off the surface and set it on dry, level ground. Mark the log as shown in the cutting guide.

2 Using a 1⅛in (29mm) bit, drill a hole in the midsection piece for the entrance. It should be 2in (5cm) down from the top of the log and about 1½in (4cm) deep.

3 With a reciprocating saw and a 9in (230mm) blade, make cuts #1–4, in that order, to divide the log into three sections: roof, midsection and floor.

WHAT SIZE BIRD?

This entrance size will suit all kinds of very small songbirds such as wrens.

Tip: When you are marking a log, look down from directly above to make it easier to mark straight lines. Make sure the marks are thick and clear enough to be visible.

4 Securely clamp down the midsection and, working from the top, drill six holes with a ½in (12mm) bit that is 7in (18cm) long. The holes should be in a circle roughly 1in (2.5cm) inside the outer ring of wood. Using the reciprocating saw and 9in (230mm) blade, cut between the drill holes until the centre piece comes loose and you can tap it out.

---

5 Now use a ½in (12mm) chisel and a dead-blow mallet to create a round cavity following the shape of the log. This leaves about 1in (2.5cm) of wood in a ring.

Chisel out the insides so that you are left with a 1in (2.5cm) thick ring of wood.

JOINING THE PIECES

6 Brush off the three sections. With a small brush, put an even coat of glue on the top of the floor section and the bottom of the midsection. Press the pieces firmly together until the seam is tight. The glue will ooze out a little.

7 Fasten the two pieces together using 2in (50mm) finish nails in a crisscross fashion (page 21). Roughly eight nails evenly spaced around the log will suffice. Place two handfuls of sawdust or wood shavings into the cavity.

8 Evenly spread glue over the top of the end grain on the midsection and the inside of the roof section. Press the pieces firmly together and fasten with 2in (50mm) finish nails in a crisscross fashion.

9 Wipe off the excess glue by rubbing sawdust briskly into all seams, all around the log. This helps to hide the seams.

Tip: Rubbing sawdust into the seams after gluing will fill any gaps, and give a more professional look.

FINISHING

10 Using a $\frac{3}{16}$in (5mm) drill bit that is 6in (15cm) long, make a hole in each side of the log that runs the entire length and exits out the top. The holes will be used to string the hanging wire through. They should not enter the internal cavity. With the same bit, drill a hole in the centre of the floor section of the birdhouse for drainage.

---

11 Make a 3ft (90cm) length of twisted PVC-coated wire, insert the ends up through the holes made in Step 10 and form a releasable loop on top (page 23). Coat the top and bottom surfaces with glue so that all end grain is saturated. Hang overnight to allow the glue to cure properly.

Hang the birdhouse overnight to allow the glue to cure properly before applying any decoration materials.

---

12 Decorate using moss, cones, bark and sticks. Take care not to penetrate the cavity with your nails. Use the roof and floor sections as your attachment points whenever possible.

Alpine Birdhouse

The Alpine design is our most popular birdhouse style. It is simple and natural, and a perfect next step from the Flat-top Birdhouse (page 32) in learning to work with round wood. While it still resembles a log, the peaked roof makes the Alpine look more like a traditional house. The softwood hollowing technique makes this one even easier for a home project.

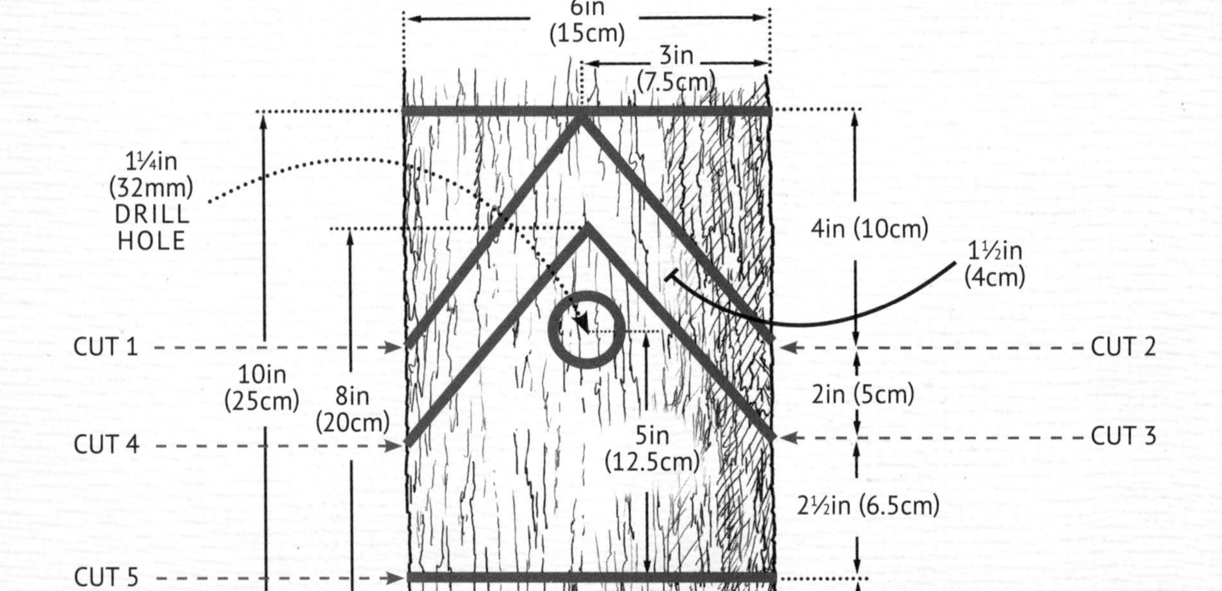

CUTTING THE LOG

1 Find a piece of deadwood about 6in (15cm) in diameter. Mark the log into three sections: roof, midsection and floor, according to the sketches.

2 With a reciprocating saw and a 9in (230mm) blade, make cuts #1 and #2 to create the peak of the roof. Cut along the inside of the roof (cuts #3 and #4). Remove the roof section and mark its top with a directional arrow. The head of the arrow should point in the direction where the entrance hole will be on the front of the midsection of the birdhouse.

3 The remaining log now contains the midsection that will become the cavity and another section that will become the floor. Make cuts #5 and #6.

HOUSE COMPONENTS

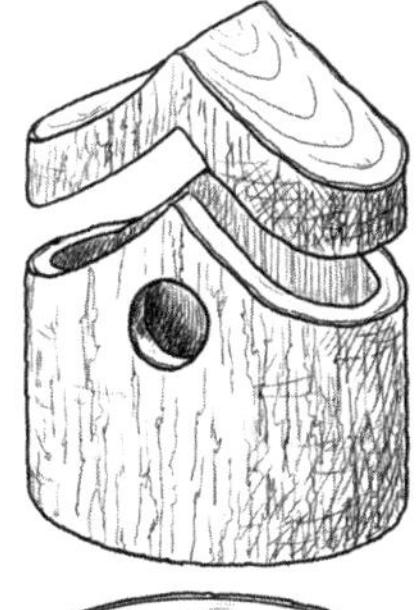

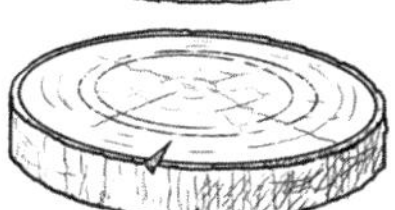

Mark the front of each piece with an arrow as you cut it to help when assembling the birdhouse later on.

Tip: Try not to cut over the same area more than once. This will ensure that all the pieces will fit back together snugly when it is time to reassemble.

4 Use a 1¼in (32mm) paddle bit to bore out the entrance hole. Now you are ready to hollow out the midsection. Using a drill with a 1½in (38mm) sharp auger bit, drill a hole in the centre of the log all the way through to the other side, creating a tunnel.

5 Stand the log upright. Using a dead-blow mallet and a ½in (12mm) chisel, begin chiselling out the centre wood. Break the pieces towards the centre of the log and remove them, until roughly 1in (2.5cm) of wood is left on the outside ring.

WHAT SIZE BIRD?

The 1¼in (32mm) entrance is the perfect size for Nuthatches (Red-breasted Nuthatch shown) and small woodpeckers.

JOINING THE PIECES

6 Brush off the three sections. With a small brush, put an even coat of glue on the top of the floor section and the bottom of the midsection. Press firmly together until the seam is tight. The glue should ooze out a little at this point.

7 Fasten the two pieces together using 2in (50mm) finish nails in a crisscross fashion (page 21). Roughly eight nails evenly spaced around the log will suffice. Place two handfuls of sawdust or wood shavings into the cavity.

8 Evenly spread glue over the top of the end grain on the midsection and the inside of the roof section. Press the pieces firmly together and fasten with 2in (50mm) finish nails in a crisscross fashion.

9 Wipe off the excess glue by rubbing sawdust briskly into all seams all around the log.

Moss can be tucked into the edges before gluing and nailing to hide any gaps.

FINISHING

10 Using a $\frac{3}{16}$in (5mm) drill bit that is 6in (15cm) long, make a hole in each side of the log that runs the entire length and exits out the top. The holes will be used to string the hanging wire through. They should not enter the internal cavity. With the same bit, drill a drain hole in the centre of the floor section of the birdhouse.

11 Make a 3ft (90cm) length of twisted PVC-coated wire, insert the ends up through the holes made in Step 10 and form a releasable loop on top (page 23). Coat the top and bottom surfaces with glue so that all end grain is saturated. Hang overnight to allow the glue to cure properly.

12 Decorate as you wish. Create the roof by placing pieces of bark over the bare wood in a vertical fashion. Attach a few sticks for decoration, perches and camouflage. Take care not to penetrate the cavity by using nails that are too long. Use the roof and floor sections as your attachment points whenever possible.

Tip: Decorating with pinecones and moss is a good way of adding elements that are also useful to the birds.

Alpine Landscape

This project creates a landscaped garden around an Alpine-style house, using sticks for trees, pinecones for bushes and mosses for garden plantings. The garden is not only charming, but also provides an area for fledging babies to land if they tumble trying to fly for the first time.

CUTTING GUIDE

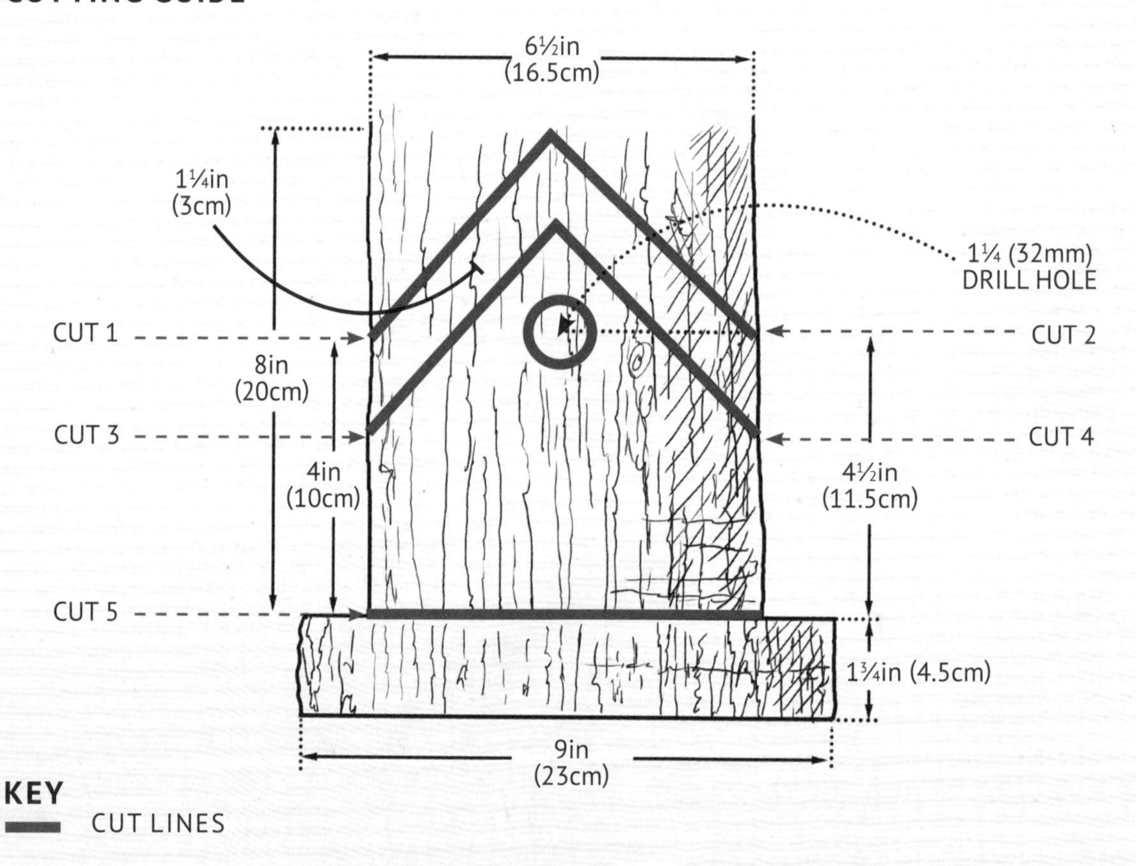

KEY

CUT LINES

MAKING THE HOUSE

1 You will need two sections of birdhouse wood. One should be 6½in (16.5cm) in diameter and 12in (30cm) long; the second should be 9in (23cm) in diameter and 1¾in (4.5cm) long. Mark the 6½in (16.5cm) log based on the cutting guide.

2 With a reciprocating saw and a 9in (230mm) blade, make cuts #1–5. Drill out the entrance hole with a 1¼in (32mm) auger bit, about 2in (5cm) deep. If the wood is relatively soft, hollow out the midsection as for Project 2 (page 40). If the wood is hard, follow the hollowing steps for Project 1 (page 34).

3 Brush off the 9in (23cm) slab and apply glue all over the surface. Then glue the bottom of the midsection and attach it to the slab with 2in (50mm) finish nails in a crisscross fashion (page 21). Add a handful of sawdust or wood shavings into the cavity. Apply glue to the roof and nail it in place.

4 Using a ¼in (6mm) bit, drill through the bottom slab on either side of the log. The holes need to line up with the side edges of the birdhouse, so that the hanging wire will run up and alongside the house. Using the same bit, drill a drain hole in the centre of the floor, just until it penetrates the cavity.

5 Run a hanging wire up through the side holes and form a releasable loop on top (page 23). Coat the top and bottom surfaces with glue. Hang overnight to allow the glue to cure properly. Decorate by adding moss all the way around to create a lawn. Use pinecones and bark nubs for shrubs and sticks for trees. Attach sticks to the outside edges of the slab as well as against the body of the birdhouse to create more depth.

HOUSE COMPONENTS

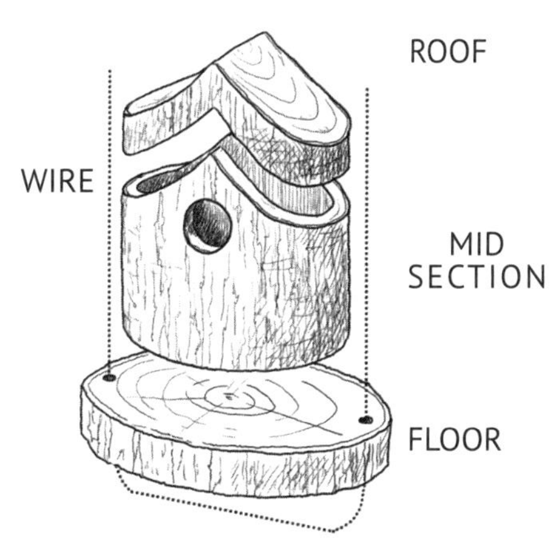

Chalet Birdhouse

In this project, the log is cut to expose the entire front of the house, which is then sanded and waxed to a protective patina. Cutting the front of the house also creates a front lawn area for you to decorate imaginatively.

HOUSE COMPONENTS

ROOF

MID SECTION

FLOOR

CUTTING GUIDE: FRONT

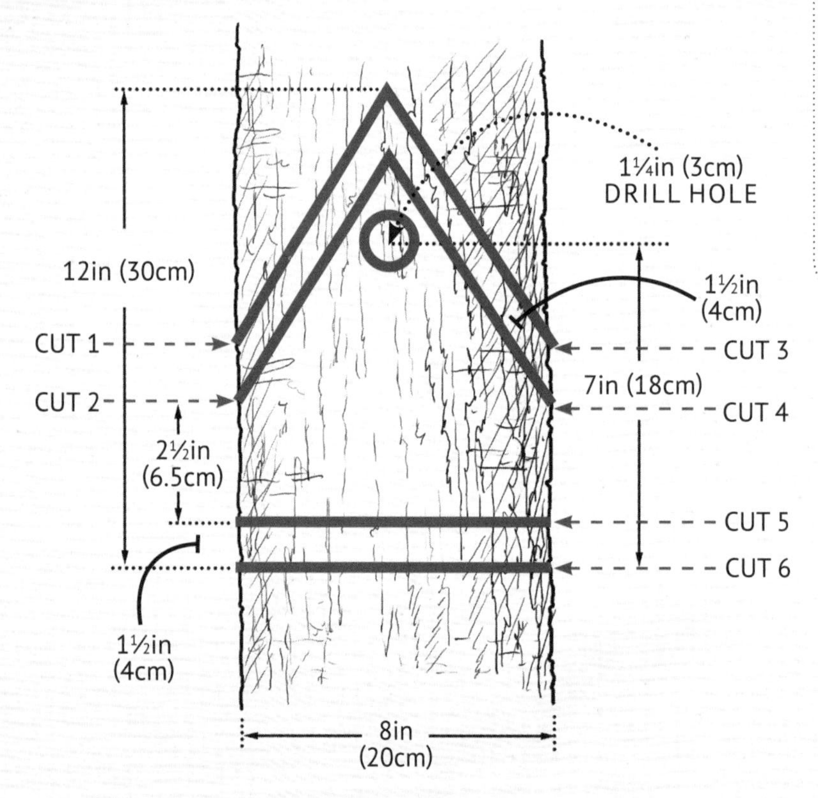

CUTTING GUIDE: SIDE

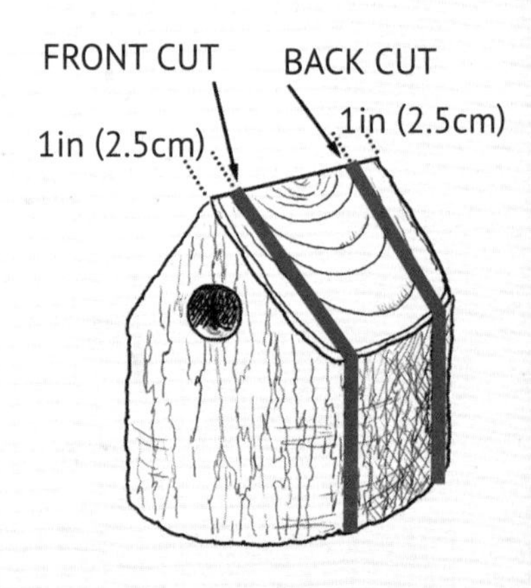

KEY

CUT LINES

CUTTING THE LOG

Strap down the log with the front face down and the back uppermost.

1 Find a good piece of birdhouse wood about 8in (20cm) in diameter and at least 15in (38cm) long. Following the front cutting guide, mark the cut lines, then make cuts #1–6 to create the roof, midsection and floor of the birdhouse.

---

2 Refer to the side cutting guide to mark the two cut lines at the top of the midsection, roughly 1in (2.5cm) towards the centre of the log. Using a 1¼in (32mm) bit, drill out the entrance hole about 2in (5cm) deep. With a reciprocating saw and a 9in (230mm) blade, cut along the two marked lines to remove the 'front' and 'back' pieces. Discard the front piece and save the back.

---

3 Cut a groove into the end grain with the reciprocating saw. It should be 1in (2.5cm) from the front face towards the centre of the log. Strap down the log using this notch.

4 Mark a series of lines across the top surface of the log, making sure they are about ½in (12mm) apart. Cut downwards along the marked lines. The grooves should run the entire length of the midsection, stopping just short of the strap notch line so as not to cut through the strap.

5 Stand the log right side up. Using a ½in (12mm) chisel, remove the pieces one at a time, creating a rough cavity that is missing the back. Carefully chisel away the remaining wood until the cavity is round inside and the walls are 1in (2.5cm) thick.

JOINING AND FINISHING

6 Apply glue to the back section you set aside in Step 2 and also to the edge of the midsection where the two pieces will join. Press firmly until the glue oozes out and then fasten them together with 2in (50mm) finish nails in a crisscross fashion (page 21). Use four nails in each side.

7 Sand the face of the birdhouse with 100-grit sandpaper until the woodgrain becomes visible and smooth. Dust well. Apply a mixture of beeswax and tung oil to seal the wood and protect it from splitting (page 22). This will also bring out the natural beauty of the wood itself.

Using natural materials to wax the birdhouse assures purity from toxins that could harm baby birds.

8 Glue and nail together the three sections of the birdhouse (see Project 2, page 41). Using a ¼in (6mm) bit, drill two holes up through either side of the birdhouse. Drill a third hole in the centre of the bottom for drainage. Twist a length of PVC-coated wire, run it up through the holes on the sides and form a releasable loop on top (page 23). Hang overnight to allow the glue to cure properly.

9 Attach roofing shingles and landscaping to your liking.

Deluxe Chalet

This variation of the Chalet Birdhouse (page 46) is perfect for nuthatches, sparrows and many other birds. It retains its natural log look on the back, but has an elegant silhouette all around.

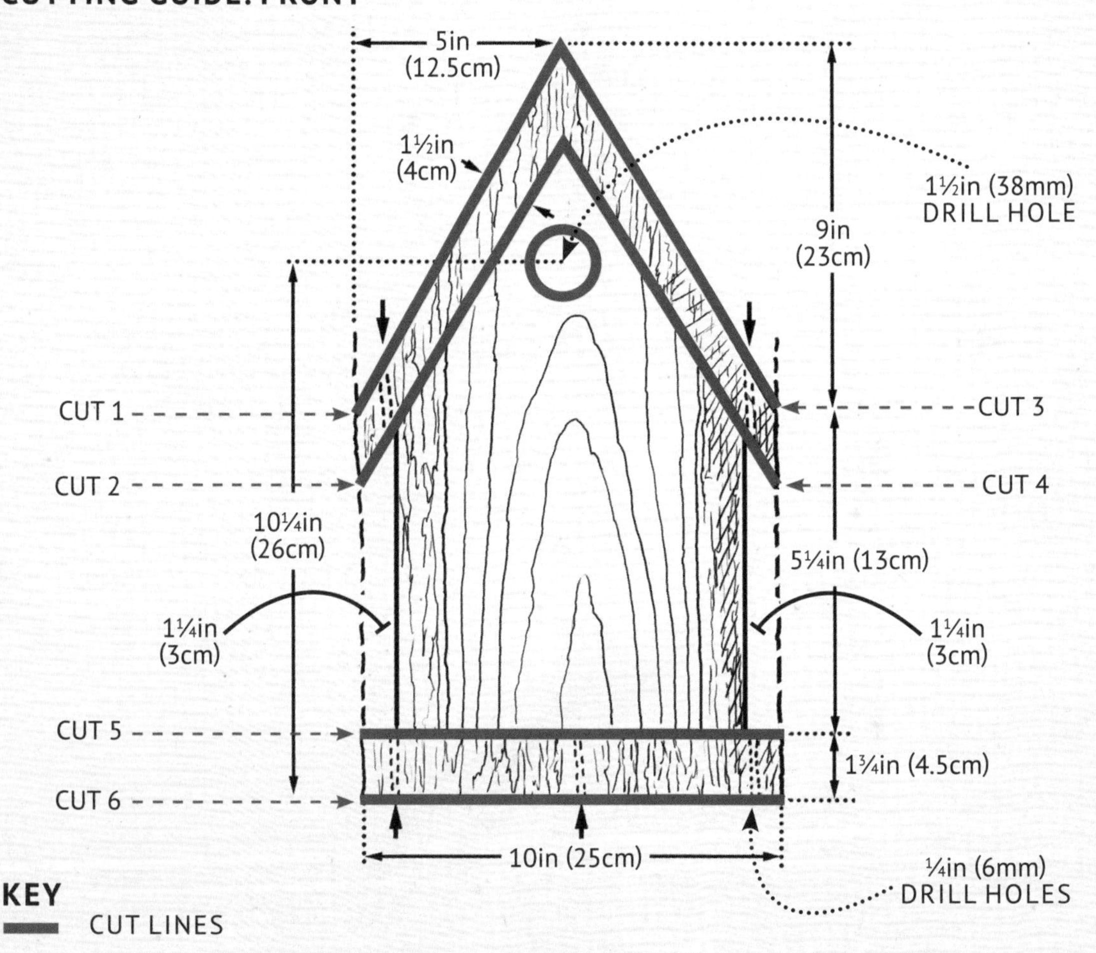

MAKING THE HOUSE

1 Find birdhouse wood that is 10in (25cm) in diameter and 20in (51cm) long. Mark the log as shown in the front cutting guide, then cut it into roof, midsection and floor pieces. Drill the entrance hole with a 1½in (38mm) drill bit, going about 3in (7.5cm) deep.

2 Stand the midsection upright and strap it down. Mark cuts #7–9, as shown in the top view cutting guide. Cut and discard these sections.

3 Hollow out the midsection, using one of the three hollowing procedures outlined in Projects 1, 2 and 4 (pages 34, 40 and 47). Sand each side to your liking. Wax and buff to protect the exposed wood (page 22).

4 Begin assembly by gluing the bottom piece thoroughly, then gluing and attaching the hollowed midsection using 2in (50mm) finish nails in a crisscross fashion (page 21). Add two handfuls of wood shavings to the cavity. Thoroughly glue the inside of the roof and the top of the hollowed house. Attach using 2in (50mm) finish nails.

5 Using a ¼in (6mm) drill bit, create wire holes on either side of the house. Drill through the bottom piece at the outside edge of the midsection and continue through the roof. Drill a third hole in the centre of the bottom for drainage. Run a hanging wire up through the side holes and form a releasable loop on top (page 23). Coat top and bottom with glue. Hang overnight to allow the glue to cure properly, then decorate.

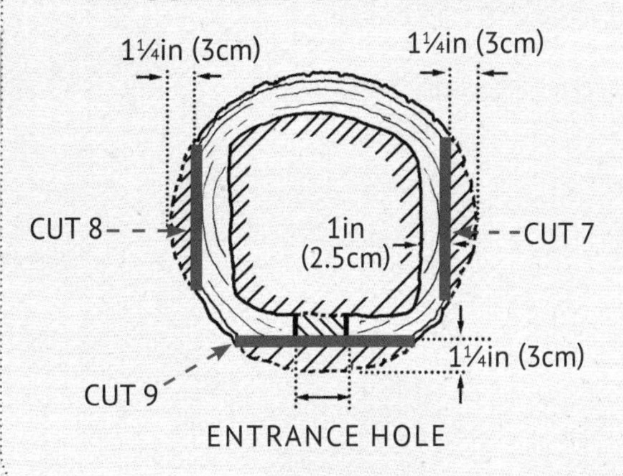

Very little sanding makes for a rustic look, whereas a very fine sanding makes for a very refined fancy Chalet.

Chalet Apartments

This is a fun project that makes a small block of 'apartments' comprising two separate birdhouses in the same log. The Chalet Apartments project makes a particularly beautiful presentation on the Tree Stand (page 86).

Variation:
You can use the basic technique explained here to make a log-shaped design (see also page 57).

HOUSE COMPONENTS

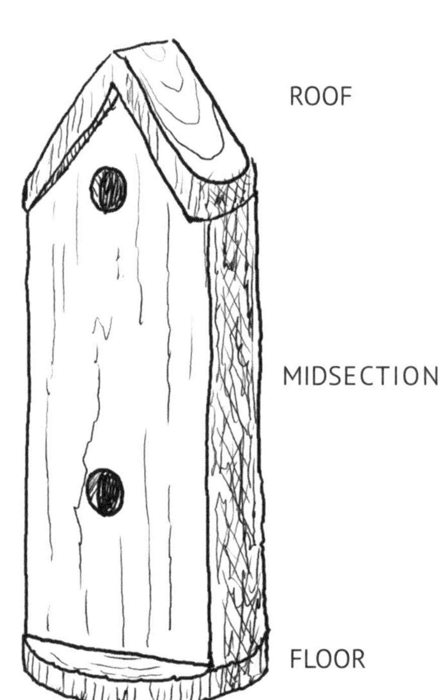

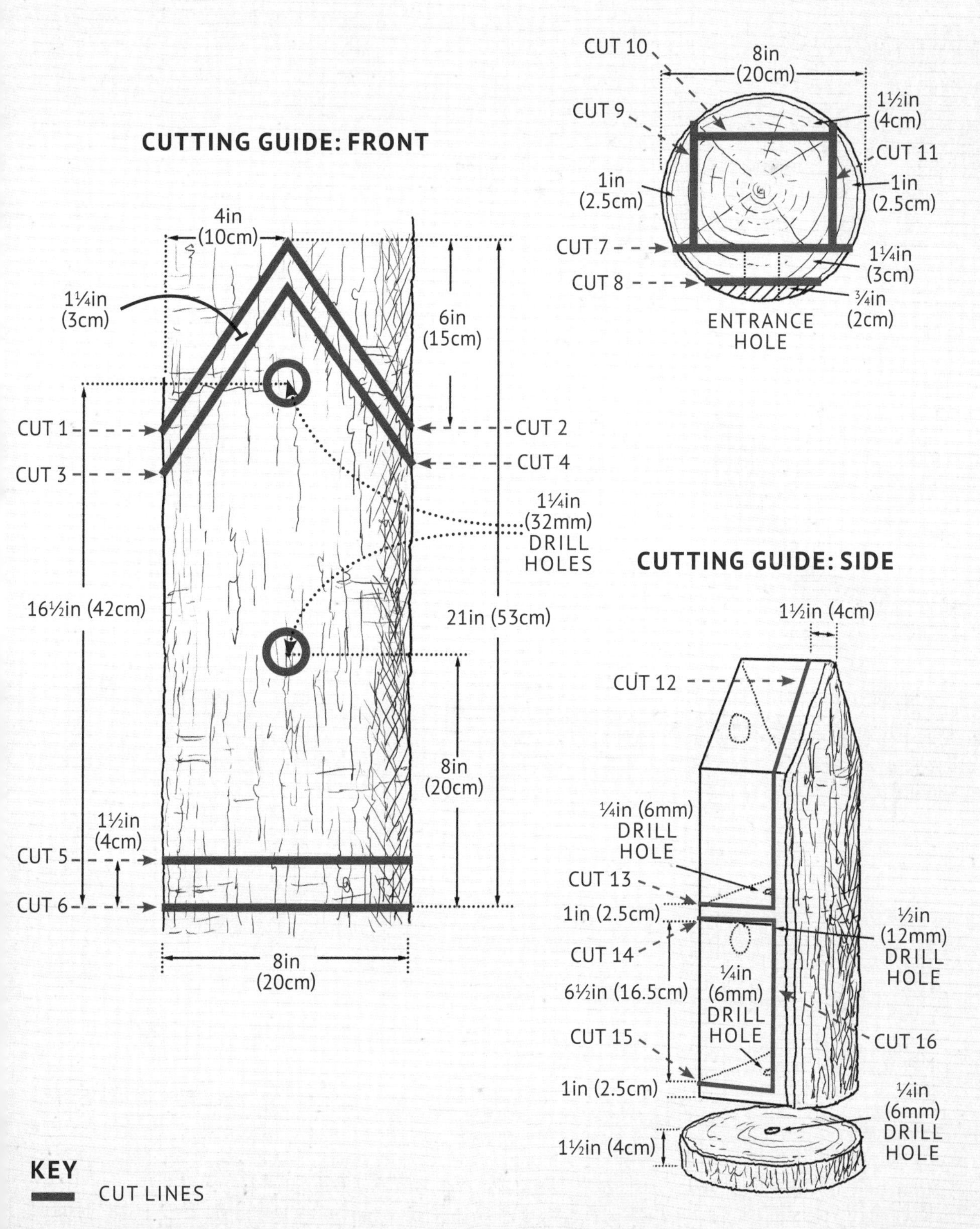
CUTTING GUIDE: FRONT
4in
(10cm)
1¼in
(3cm)
6in
(15cm)
CUT 1
CUT 2
CUT 3
CUT 4
1¼in
(32mm)
DRILL
HOLES
16½in (42cm)
21in (53cm)
8in
(20cm)
1½in
(4cm)
CUT 5
CUT 6
8in
(20cm)
CUTTING GUIDE: TOP VIEW
CUT 10
8in
(20cm)
CUT 9
1½in
(4cm)
CUT 11
1in
(2.5cm)
1in
(2.5cm)
CUT 7
1¼in
(3cm)
CUT 8
¾in
(2cm)
ENTRANCE
HOLE
CUTTING GUIDE: SIDE
1½in (4cm)
CUT 12
¼in (6mm)
DRILL
HOLE
CUT 13
1in (2.5cm)
½in
(12mm)
DRILL
HOLE
CUT 14
6½in (16.5cm)
¼in
(6mm)
DRILL
HOLE
CUT 15
CUT 16
1in (2.5cm)
¼in
(6mm)
DRILL
HOLE
1½in (4cm)
KEY
CUT LINES

CUTTING THE LOG

1 Find a piece of good birdhouse wood that is 8in (20cm) in diameter and 24in (61cm) long. Mark the initial cut lines and two entrance holes on your log as shown in the front cutting guide. Make cuts #1–6 to make the roof, midsection and floor.

It is very important for reassembly that the cuts are made in the order they are numbered.

---

2 Using a 1¼in (32mm) bit, drill the two entrance holes about 2in (5cm) deep into the midsection.

---

3 Stand the midsection upright and mark the top of it according to the top cutting guide. Make cuts #7–11. At this point, you should be left with a midsection that is square on three sides and round on the back.

---

4 Lay the midsection down on its side. Use the side cutting guide to mark cut lines #12–16. Using a ½in (12mm) bit, drill a hole all the way through the midsection at the intersection of cut lines #14 and #16.

---

5 Strap the midsection down and make cuts #12–15. At cut #16, start by plunging the saw blade into the drill hole and then cut downwards. Remove the two centre pieces you have just cut out and save them to make roof shingles.

JOINING THE PIECES

6 Begin reassembly. Glue the bottom of the midsection to the top of the floor section. Nail together in a crisscross pattern (page 21). Four 2in (50mm) finish nails are sufficient for now.

7 Using a ¼in (6mm) bit, drill two drain holes as shown in the side cutting guide. One hole should go up through the middle of the floor section and the base of the midsection. The other hole should go through the middle of the 'shelf' that will form the floor of the upper cavity of the birdhouse.

8 Sand the face of the birdhouse to your liking, then rub with wax and tung oil mixture (page 22). Next reattach the right and the left sides by gluing and nailing together in a crisscross fashion. After all the pieces are assembled, attach the face in the same way.

9 Glue and nail the roof to the birdhouse as before. Rub sawdust into all the seams of the house.

Rub sawdust into the seams to fill any gaps and spaces for a professional and uniform look.

WHAT SIZE BIRD?

This house will attract birds like house sparrows and the common redstart (see page 56). In the USA we see social songbirds like the black-capped chickadee living in groups like this in the wild.

FINISHING

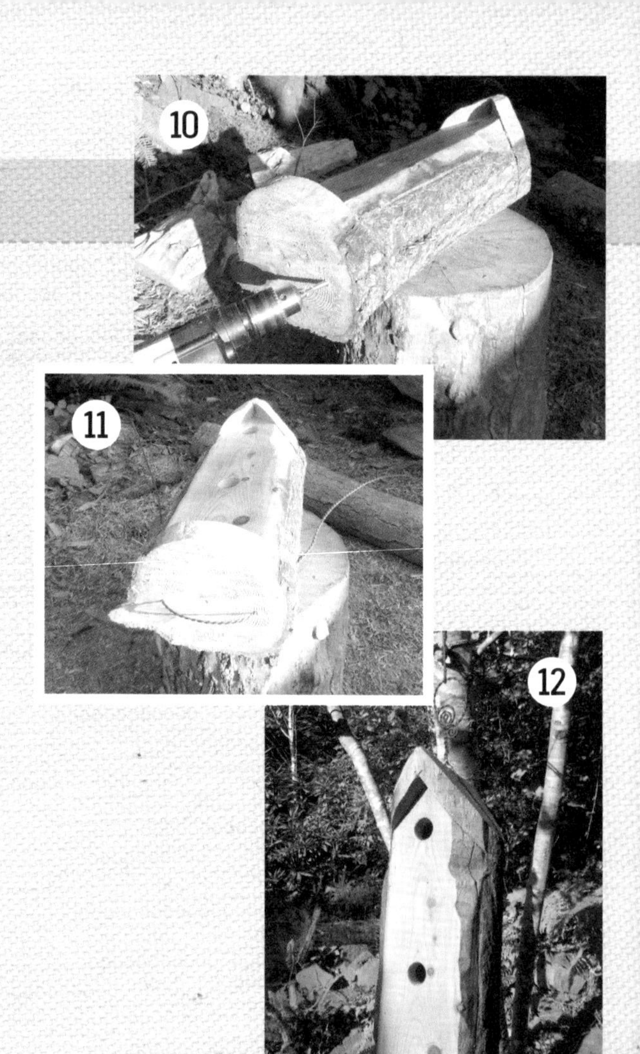

10 Using a ¼in (6mm) drill bit that is 8in (20cm) long, make two wire holes up through the floor section of the birdhouse. Start the drill holes about 1in (2.5cm) inwards from the sides and angle outwards and upwards.

11 Insert a length of twisted PVC-coated wire up through the holes and around the whole birdhouse, forming a releasable loop on top (page 23).

12 Coat the top and bottom surfaces of the house with glue to saturate the end grain. Hang to dry overnight.

13 Put some wood shavings and sawdust into each cavity. Decorate according to your liking, using 2in (50mm) nails to attach the pieces. Make up your own custom design or use the decorations on the birdhouse shown here for inspiration.

This birdhouse suits birds around the world including the common redstart.

End-piece Birdhouse

This birdhouse style creates a dramatic effect when placed against any backdrop. If the wood is weathered to a silver patina, it makes an especially nice contrast to greenery found in your garden or the blue sky beyond your balcony. Keep your eye out for interesting shapes, protruding branch remnants and knotholes.

CUTTING GUIDE

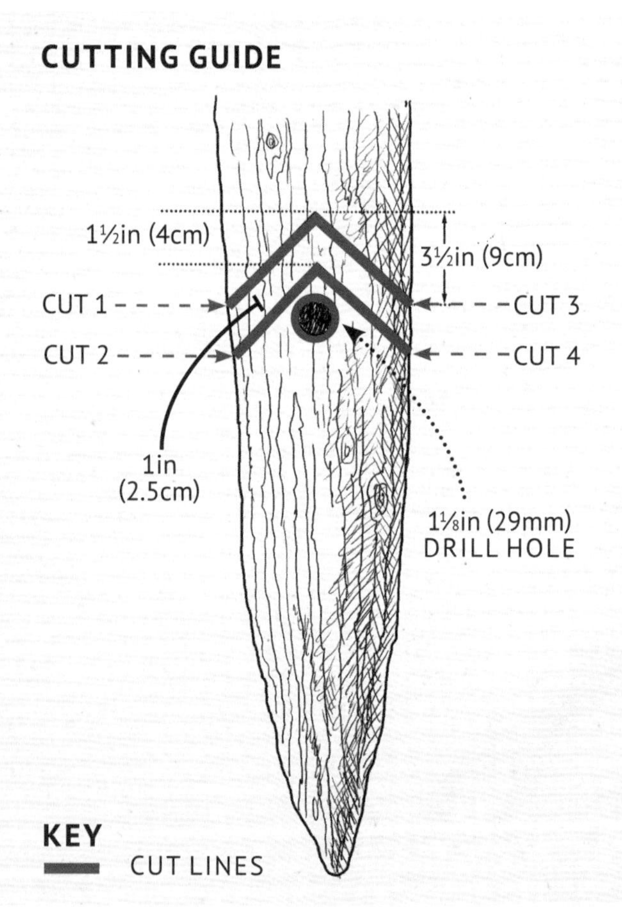

INTERIOR CAVITY

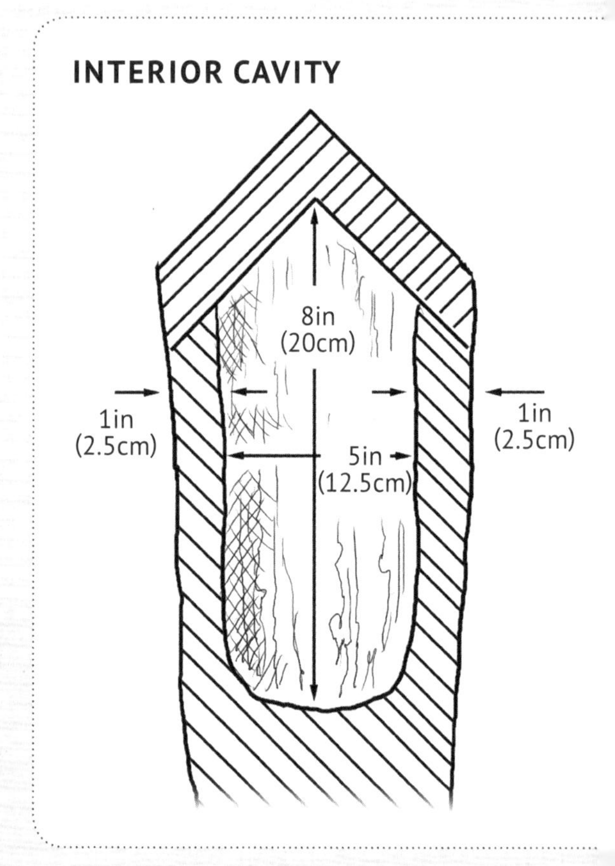

CUTTING THE LOG

1 Find birdhouse wood at least 7in (18cm) in diameter at one end and at least 16in (40cm) long before tapering off. Strap or clamp your piece at a point before its natural taper begins. This prevents the tapered wood from slipping out while you work with it.

2 Mark cut lines #1–4 as shown in the cutting guide. Make the cuts, remove the peaked roof section and set aside.

3 Using a 1⅛in (29mm) bit, drill the entrance hole. It should be positioned about ¾in (2cm) down from the peaked top of the log and about 1½in (4cm) deep.

4 Using a 1½in (38mm) auger bit, drill down through the centre of the log. Start in the middle and drill down to about 8in (20cm) from the peak of the cavity section.

5 Chisel back the sides, widening slowly as you go. Make sure the exterior walls are at least ¾in (2cm) thick or thicker when finished.

Tip: Be wary of logs that have deep splits. This means that sap was trapped inside and that the log will fall apart when you try to work with it.

JOINING AND FINISHING

6 Add some wood chips back into the cavity you have just created. Attach the roof piece with glue and nails in a crisscross fashion (page 21).

7 Make a drain hole in the back with a ¼in (6mm) drill bit. Start below the cavity and drill up at a 45-degree angle just until you feel the bit penetrating the inside of the cavity.

8 Using a ¼in (6mm) bit, drill holes for the hanging wire. Start at the centre of the roofline, roughly ½in (12mm) in from the edge, and angle the bit towards the back so that the exit is about 5in (12.5cm) down from where you started. These holes can go above or below the drain hole.

9 Make a 3ft (90cm) length of twisted PVC-coated wire, insert the ends up through the holes made in Step 8 and form a releasable loop on top (page 23).

10 Glue the top of the roof to coat the end grain and hang to dry overnight. Decorate using your imagination or look at the example shown here for inspiration.

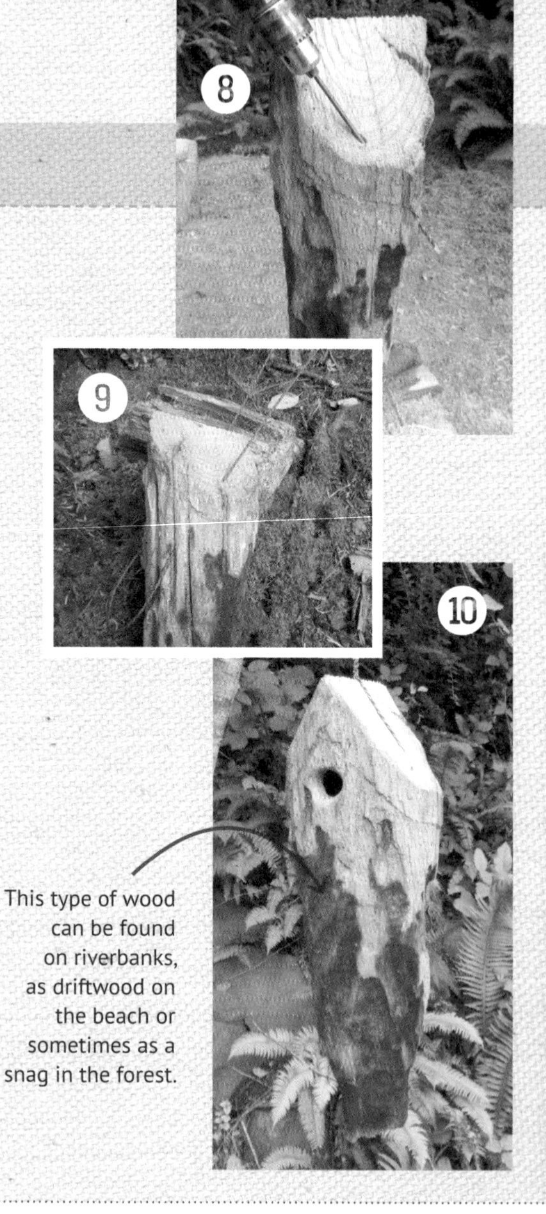

This type of wood can be found on riverbanks, as driftwood on the beach or sometimes as a snag in the forest.

WHAT SIZE BIRD?

This nestbox is suitable for songbirds, such as titmice: great titmice in the UK and Europe, tufted in the south-east USA, and juniper in the south-west USA.

Tip: Based on the dimensions given, this house is songbird size and will attract any of those birds.

Flat-backed Birdhouse Set

This is a fun project for your own garden or to share with loved ones, since it makes two usable birdhouses out of one piece of wood. They can be decorated as a twin set, or as differently as your imagination can dream up.

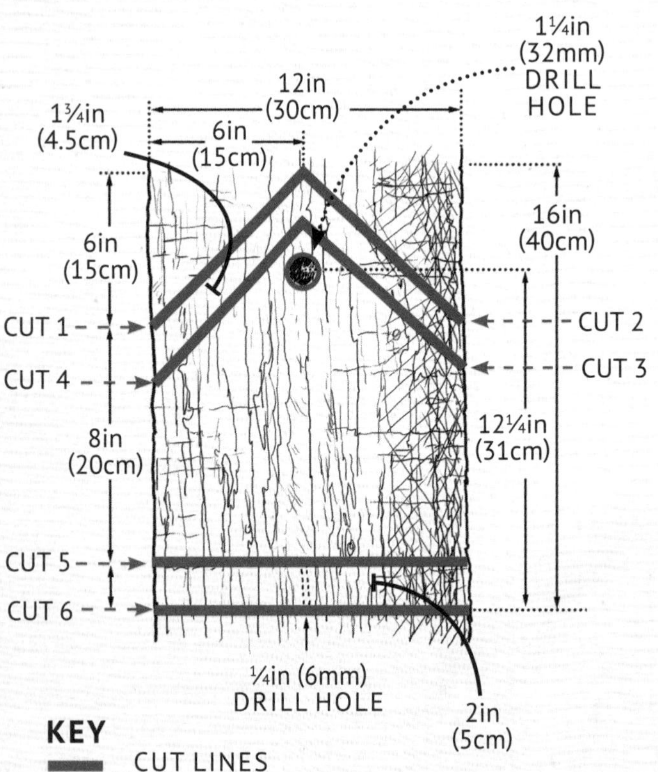

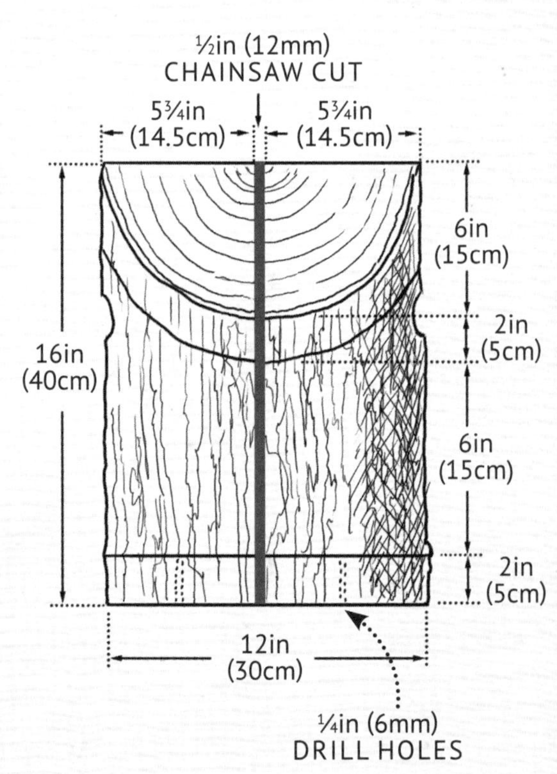

CUTTING THE LOG

1 Find a birdhouse log 12in (30cm) in diameter and approximately 20in (51cm) long. Referring to the front cutting guide, mark cut lines #1–6 on the log. Make cuts #1 and #2, creating the roof shape. Also make cut #6, creating the bottom of the floor.

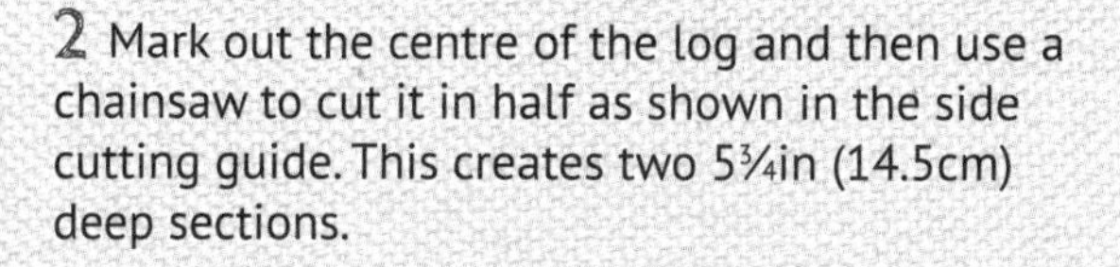

2 Mark out the centre of the log and then use a chainsaw to cut it in half as shown in the side cutting guide. This creates two 5¾in (14.5cm) deep sections.

3 Following the front cutting guide, mark the spot for the entrance hole on one of your identical log sections. Next, make the same mark on the second piece. Using a 1¼in (32mm) paddle bit, drill the entrance hole 2in (5cm) deep on both birdhouses.

4 Make cuts #3–5 on one log and then repeat on the other. This creates three sections for each house: roof, midsection and floor.

These two houses are made of drifted cedar wood. Notice how each side of the log has weathered to a different colour.

5 Now hollow out both identical midsections, using the technique described for Project 2 (page 40). Using a ¼in (6mm) bit, drill a drain hole in the centre of each floor piece.

JOINING AND FINISHING

6 Reattach the birdhouse pieces by starting with one floor and attaching its midsection with glue and crisscrossing 2in (50mm) finish nails (page 21). Fill the cavity with a handful of wood shavings and then glue and attach its roof piece with 2in (50mm) nails. When you finish one house, repeat these steps on the other.

7 Decide how you want the birdhouses to hang. We have added a twisted wire loop on the back of each house (page 122). Alternatively, using a ¼in (6mm) bit, drill two holes up through either side of each birdhouse, run a length of twisted wire up through the holes and form a releasable loop on top (page 23).

8 Coat the top and bottom of both houses with glue and hang to dry overnight. Now choose a decorating style to embellish your houses with bird-friendly elements. Your area's pinecones, spruce cones and fir cones all contain seeds that wild birds depend on eating. The mosses and sticks in your area make great camouflage.

Sometimes sharing the same tree to build projects connects us to each other and can even work to close the geographical divide between modern families: keep one house from the set and pass the other as a gift to your loved ones.

WHAT SIZE BIRD?

Small woodpeckers, such as downy in North America (shown here) and lesser spotted in Europe, will be attracted to this box.

Group Swallow House

This house is perfect for grouping birds such as swallows and martins. The house needs to be mounted 6-12ft (1.8-3.7m) above the ground on a post or on our Tree Stand (page 86). It includes a removable face so that you can clean out all four houses in one action.

CUTTING GUIDE: FRONT

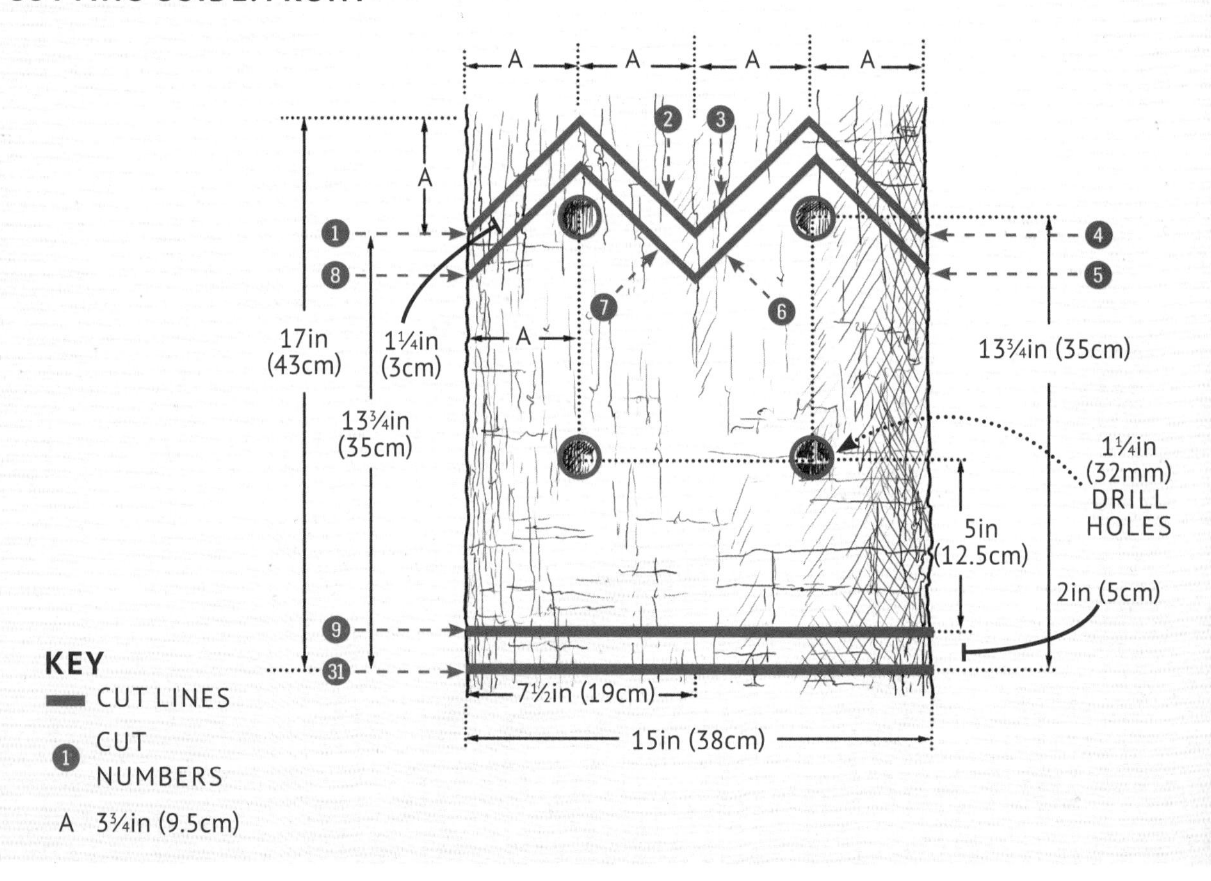

CUTTING GUIDE: TOP VIEW

13in (33cm)
12 3½in (9cm) DEEP
17 15 18 16 19 20
B C
15in (38cm)
8in (20cm)
10 2in (5cm) DEEP
10in (25cm)
D
11 2in (5cm) DEEP
14 13
B C C D
9 3½in (9cm) DEEP
13in (33cm)
FRONT

KEY

CUT LINES

10 CUT NUMBERS

B 5in (12.5cm)

C 1in (2.5cm)

D 3½in (9cm)

CUTTING GUIDE: INTERIOR

21 22
15in (38cm)
E
24 26 23 25
E
5in (12.5cm)
27 30 29 28
½in (12mm)
15in (38cm)
2in (5cm)

KEY

CUT LINES

27 CUT NUMBERS

E 1in (2.5cm)

3D PLAN

3½in (9cm)
2in (5cm)

CUTTING THE LOG

1 Start with a log 15in (38cm) in diameter and 20in (51cm) long. Lay it down and mark cut lines #1–9, the four drill holes for the entrance, and cut line #31, referring to the front cutting guide. Strap down the log and make cuts #1–8, in that order, using a 12in (300mm) reciprocating saw blade. Remove the top. Using a 1¼in (32mm) bit, drill the entrance holes 3½in (9cm) deep.

2 Unstrap the log and stand it up on end. Referring to the top cutting guide, mark cut lines #11–20. It is important to make your critical measurements from the centre of the log outwards. Referring also to the 3D plan, make cut #9, 3½in (9cm) deep. Make cuts #10 and #11, 2in (5cm) deep. Make cut #12, 3½in (9cm) deep.

3 Label the exterior walls of the birdhouse and then make cuts #13–20, in that order. When you have done this, you will have removed the excess pieces of wood and created the exterior walls of the birdhouse. Sand the outside surfaces of the exterior walls to your liking and then set those walls aside for later reassembly.

4 At this point the centre of the log is still attached to the base. Refer to the interior cutting guide and mark cut lines #21–30. With the 12in (300mm) reciprocating saw blade, make cuts #21–30. Remove and save the four interior blocks for future projects. Now you have the interior walls and the floors of the birdhouses.

5 Use a ¼in (6mm) drill bit to make a drain hole in the centre of each birdhouse floor. Each hole should penetrate all the way through to provide drainage in case of heavy, directional rain.

JOINING THE PIECES

6 Glue all the end grain that is exposed, except for the very bottom of the birdhouse. Next, glue and reattach the back wall piece (from Step 3) with 2in (50mm) finish nails in a crisscross fashion (page 21). Make sure you put glue on the inside of that wall where it joins the dividing wall. Then glue and reattach the left and the right side walls.

---

7 Apply glue to the inside face of the front wall piece and all its end grain, then set aside. Then apply glue to the end of the left, centre and right walls where the front wall will reattach. Apply glue to the bottom of the roof piece. Let all these dry separately overnight.

---

8 First, apply wax to all areas that have been glued on the front wall (its inside surface and all its end grain). Also apply wax to every area the front wall will touch when reattached. This ensures that the glued pieces will not stick together in the future.

---

9 Place the face board onto the base, make a drill hole ⅛in (3mm) in diameter by 1¼in (32mm) deep and countersink it, so that the screw will sit flush to the face when you are done. Attach with a 2in (50mm) galvanised deck screw or stainless steel screw. Wax and buff all the exterior walls of the birdhouse.

---

10 Reattach the roof with 2in (50mm) nails, putting glue only where the seams will touch.

Do not let the glue ooze out when reattaching the roof; this makes for a prettier birdhouse.

FINISHING

11 Turn the birdhouse on its back and glue the top and bottom surfaces. Leave it to dry completely.

12 File the entrance holes to an oval to allow for the shoulders of swallows. They need another ¼in (6mm) on each side, making a finished dimension of 1¼in (3cm) top to bottom and 1½in (4cm) side to side. Add a handful of sawdust and wood shavings to the inside of each finished house.

---

13 Decorate to your own taste. Keep in mind that these houses need more dramatic decor since they are large to begin with and may be mounted farther from your house windows. Because the front of the house is removable for cleaning, remember not to decorate directly in front of it. If you do attach decorations to the front face, the nails should not be long enough to penetrate the wall or you may accidentally nail the face in place.

WHAT SIZE BIRD?

The 1¼in (32mm) entrance holes are suited to grouping birds like tree swallows (as shown) found in the USA, or starlings.

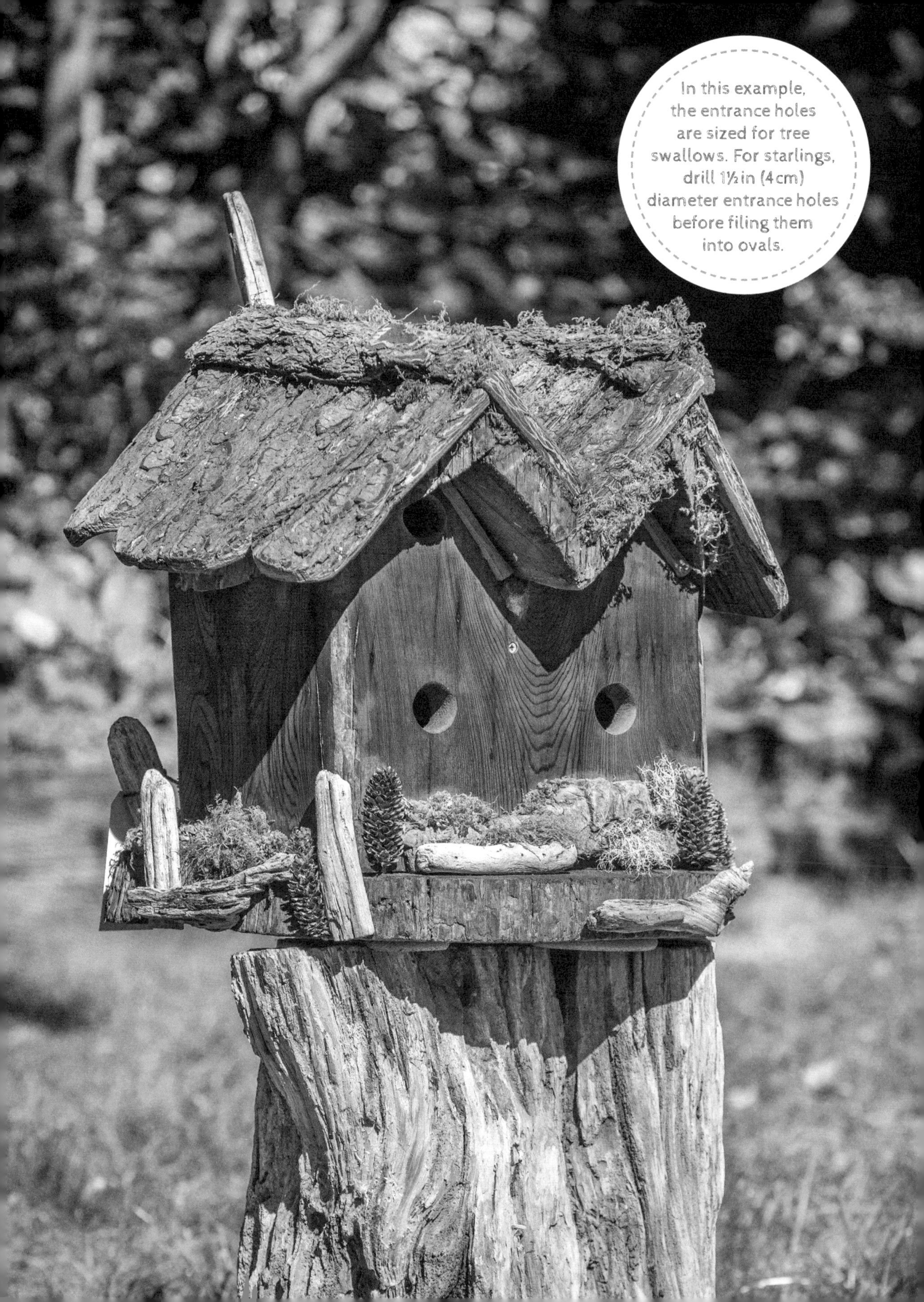

In this example, the entrance holes are sized for tree swallows. For starlings, drill 1½in (4cm) diameter entrance holes before filing them into ovals.

Rootball Birdhouse

This birdhouse is full of whimsy! Fast-growing softwood trees like alder, birch, poplar and pine make good rootballs that have great personality. Often the bark remains on them because they have been cured slowly underground. Small, naturally dead trees can often be found on river edges and coastlines or when people have cleared trees for fences or construction projects.

CUTTING GUIDE

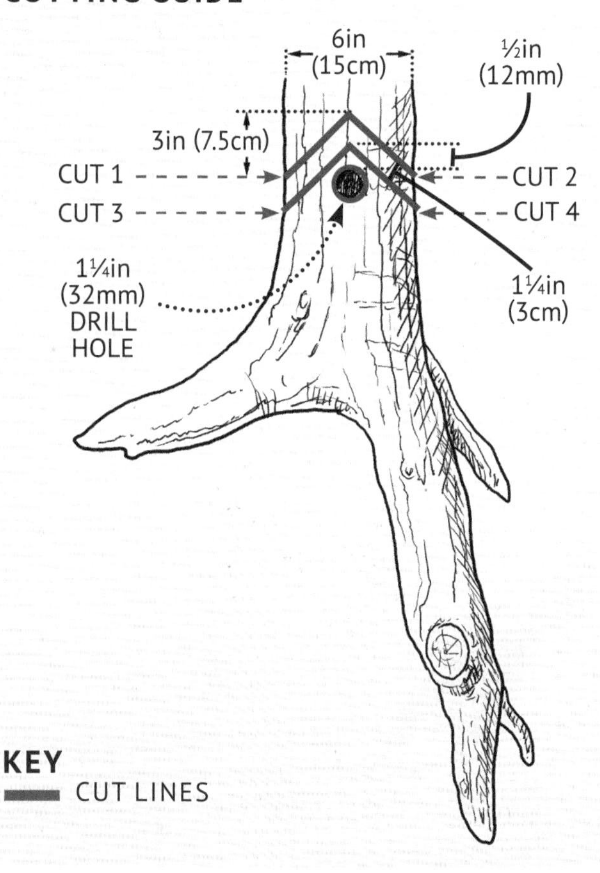

KEY

CUT LINES

INTERIOR CAVITY

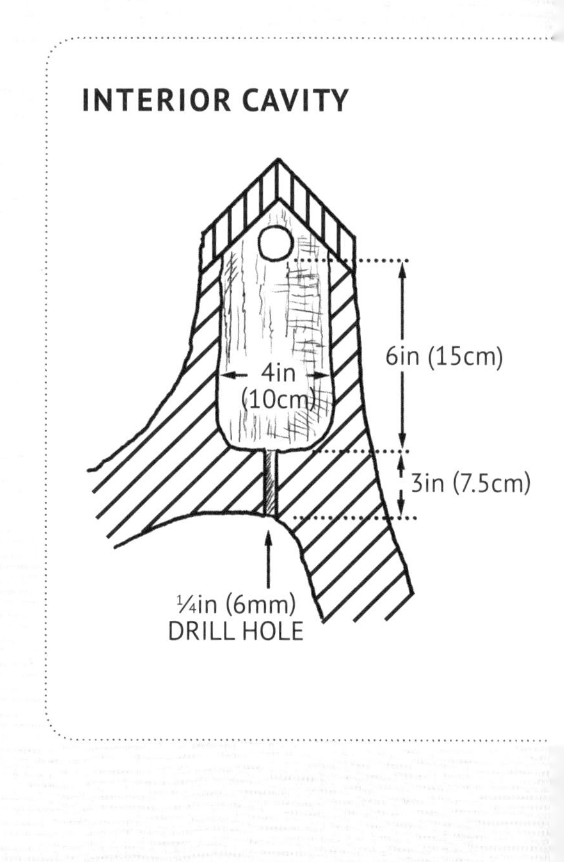

MAKING THE HOUSE

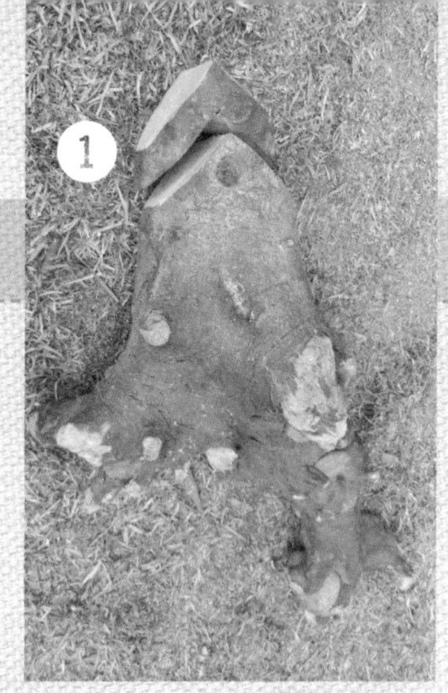

1 Find a rootball at least 6in (15cm) in diameter and 12in (30cm) long before it reaches the portion that starts to fan out into the roots. Find the centre line in the rootball and mark for the roof, according to the cutting guide, creating a roof that is 1¼in (3cm) wide. Make cuts #1–4 and set the roof piece aside. Drill out the entrance hole with a 1⅛in (29mm) bit to about 2in (5cm) deep.

2 Using a 1½in (38mm) auger bit, drill down through the middle of the end grain, following the soft centre down to a distance of about 6in (15cm). Begin chiselling out the centre wood until about 1in (2.5cm) of wood remains on the outside.

3 With the same auger bit, plunge down in a circular pattern until you create a relatively flat bottom inside the birdhouse. Using a ¼in (6mm) drill bit that is 6in (15cm) long, drill straight up the back of the rootball until you penetrate the interior of the house. This provides drainage. Glue both sides of the roof end grain, then attach the roof with 2in (50mm) finish nails in a crisscross fashion (page 21).

4 Using a drill bit ¼in (6mm) in diameter by 12in (30cm) long, drill a hole on each side of the house, run a twisted wire through the holes and form a releasable loop on top (see Project 7, page 60, for more detailed instructions). Apply glue to the top of the house and hang to dry overnight.

5 Decorate to enhance the personality of your rootball, playing up the qualities it already has. Sometimes the root tendrils look like arms, sometimes legs and other times it becomes some sort of animal. Let your imagination run wild!

Open Nester

This is a great roost for birds looking for overnight protection. It also answers housing needs for open-nesting birds. It is suitable for birds of all sizes. Here we are making one of interest to smaller open-nesting birds such as finches and sparrows. For more information on where to site an open nester, see page 27.

CUTTING GUIDE

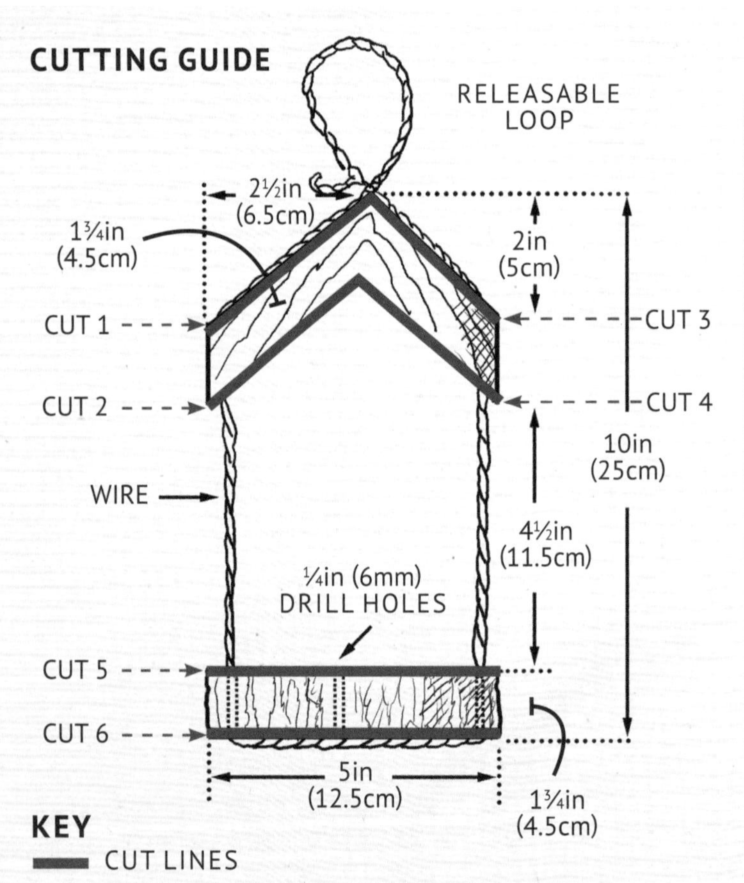

KEY

CUT LINES

GUIDE TO DRILL HOLES

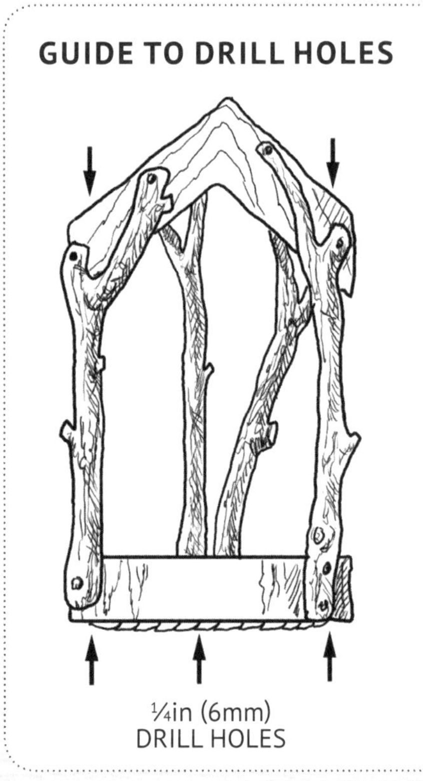

MAKING THE NESTER

1 Find birdhouse wood that is 5in (12.5cm) in diameter and about 6in (15cm) long. Using the dimensions from the cutting guide, mark cut lines #1–6 and then make those cuts. This will create the roof and the floor.

2 Find four sticks that are at least ¾in (2cm) in diameter and 10in (25cm) long. Using 2in (50mm) nails, attach the sticks on four different points of the floor and the four corresponding points on the roof above to connect the roof to the floor. Once they are in place, trim them with secateurs or a hand saw, so that they are flush with the wood.

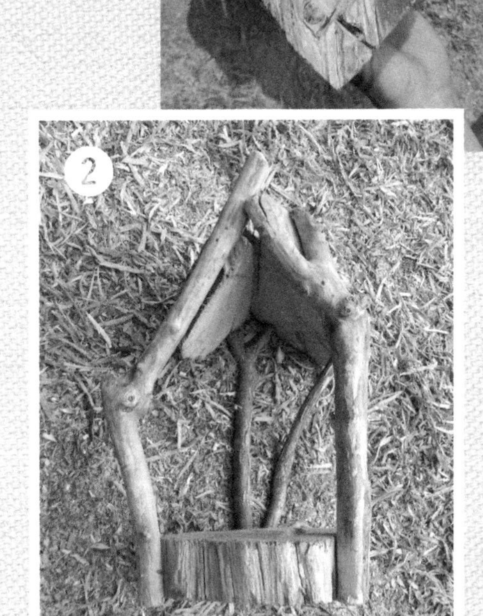

3 Using a ¼in (6mm) bit that is 12in (30cm) long, drill four holes for the wire to go through. With the same bit, make a drain hole in the centre of the floor. Thread a length of twisted wire up through the holes and form a releasable loop on top (page 23).

4 Saturate all the end grain with glue and hang to dry overnight.

5 Decorate the bottom of the nesting platform with a bed of moss. Attach the moss around the edges with spruce cones or pieces of stick. After you have done this, add the roof shingles, and then begin to decorate the structure with sticks that you think the birds will perch on.

Birds and Bees House

This project combines multiple pollinator houses and a bird habitat together. Small songbirds do not regularly eat mason bees, their eggs or pollen, so this whimsical house is of practical use to both species. There is a lot of artistic licence, depending on how you cut and decorate it, from creating a castle to a small village.

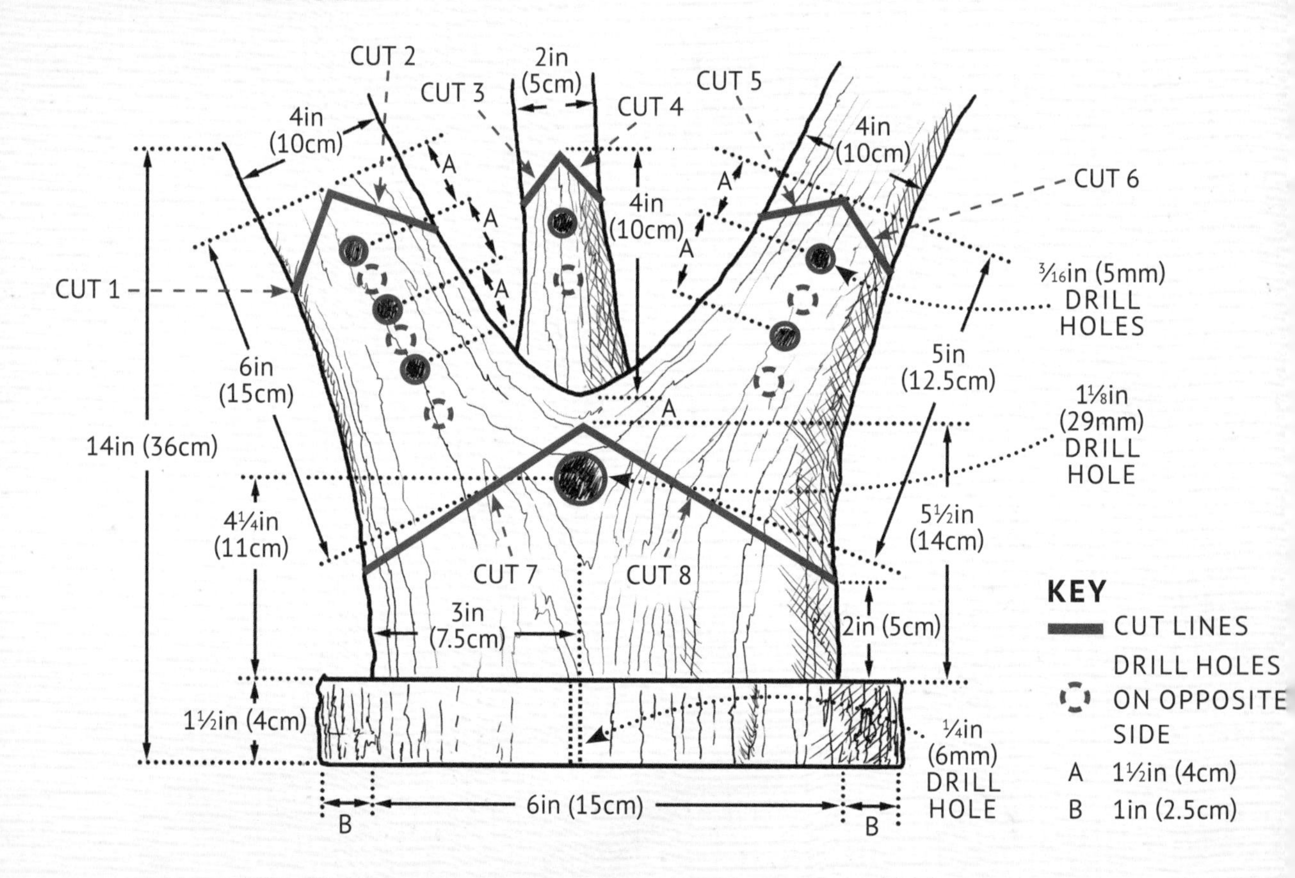

CUTTING THE LOG

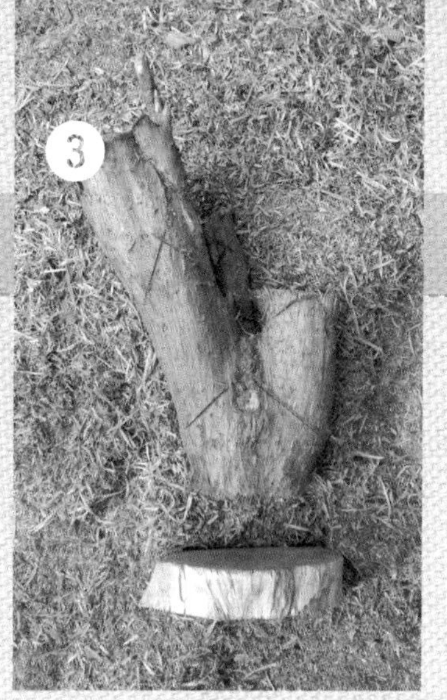

1 This house needs to be cut from a section of tree that is branching out. The main part of the log for the house should be at least 6in (15cm) in diameter. You will need at least 6in (15cm) from the bottom of the base to the beginning of the branching. The length of the branches themselves should be at least 4–6in (10–15cm). A total log length of 14–16in (36–40cm) would be good for this project. (Look carefully at the sketch to get an idea of what shape and qualities you are looking for.)

2 You will also need a bigger slice of wood for the house to sit on. This will become its 'garden'. The slice should be about 8in (20cm) in diameter and 1½in (4cm) thick. It can be driftwood or forest wood and needs to be well cured.

3 Strap the log down and mark cut lines #1–8 according to the cutting guide. Mark the entrance hole with a 1⅛in (29mm) paddle bit; this will help you visualise the birdhouse within the other house peaks.

4 Using a reciprocating saw with a 12in (300mm) blade, make cuts #1–8, in the order they are shown. Using a 1⅛in (29mm) bit, drill the entrance hole about 3in (7.5cm) deep.

5 Set aside the roof section for later. Strap down the midsection and hollow it out. If the wood you have found is relatively soft, hollow out as for Project 2 (page 40). If the wood is hard, follow the steps for Project 1 (page 34).

JOINING AND FINISHING

6 Apply glue to the end grain of the midsection and the top of the slice that will form the garden. Attach them using 2in (50mm) nails in a crisscross fashion (page 21). Put a handful of wood shavings inside the cavity of the midsection. Glue and reattach the roof.

7 Using a 3⁄16in (5mm) bit, drill all of the pollinator holes. You have freedom here to decide how to space the pollinator chambers or use the exact dimensions from the sketch.

8 Using a ¼in (6mm) drill bit, make a drain hole in the bottom centre of the slice for the birdhouse floor. Following the sketch opposite, drill the four holes for the wiring. Thread a length of twisted PVC-coated wire up through the holes and form a releasable loop on top (page 23).

9 Coat the top peaks and bottom of the birdhouse thoroughly with glue and hang to dry overnight.

10 Decorate the house as you wish. For example, roofing the peaks in the same style as each other will create the look of a castle; roofing the peaks in different styles will give the look of a rustic village.

WIRING

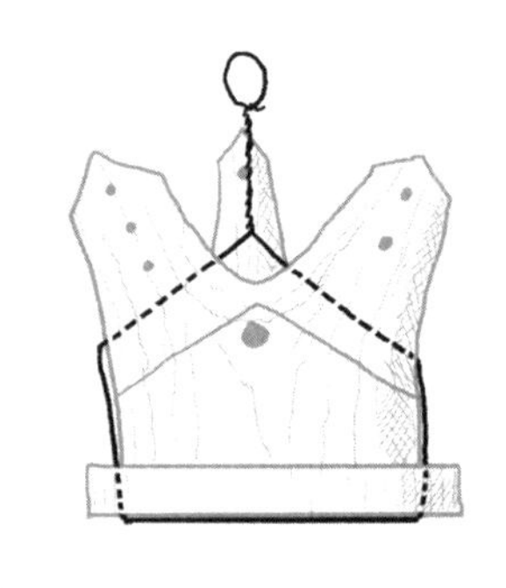

You may want to use a marker, dark paint or a woodburner to darken the pollinator holes, giving the illusion that they are hollow like the birdhouse. This does not affect their function.

Owl House with Clean-out

This delightful house will attract owls of all kinds depending on your location, plus many other birds such as kingfishers. There is room for all sorts of other inhabitants and the unique clean-out enables you to evacuate a squirrel, mouse or wasp nest if necessary - make sure that you avoid disturbing any birds.

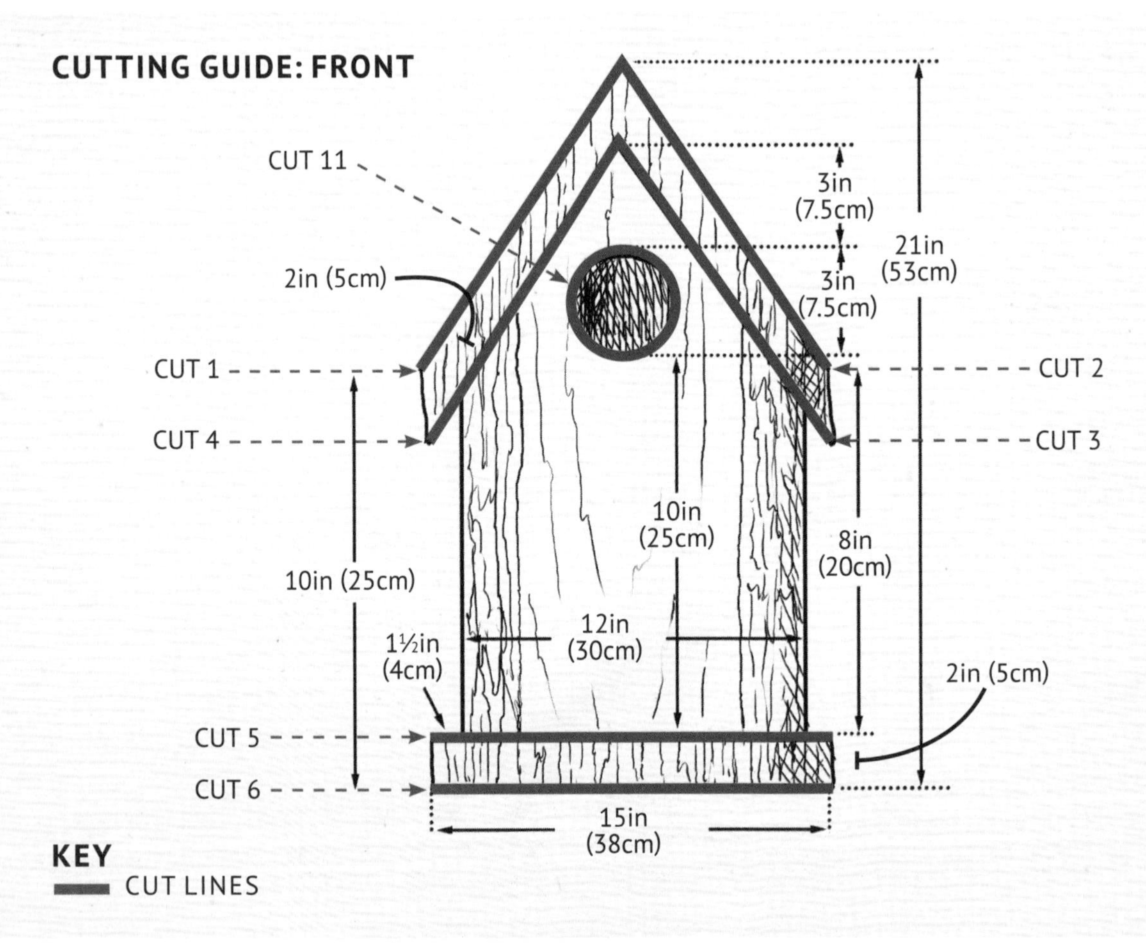

CUTTING GUIDE: BACK

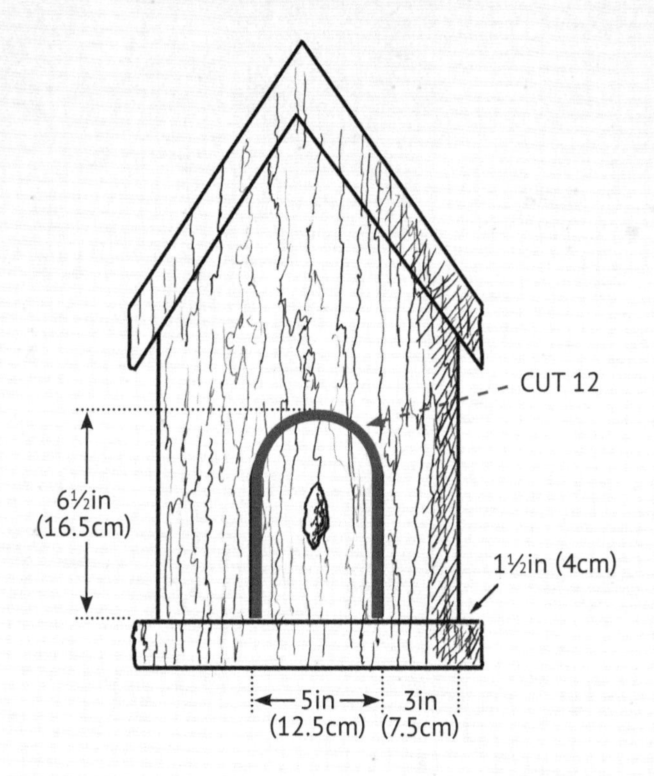

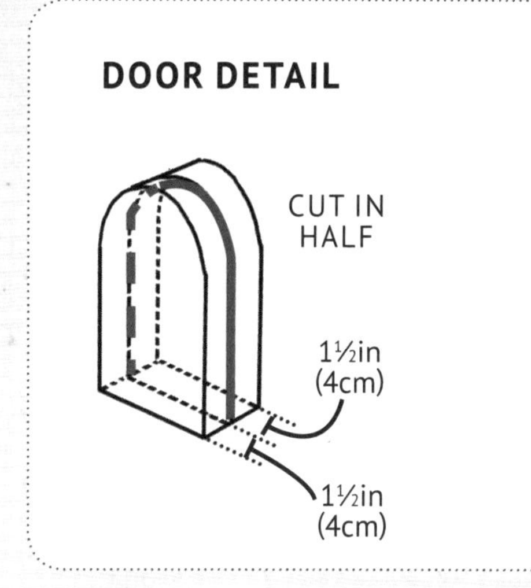

CUTTING GUIDE: TOP VIEW

5in
(12.5cm)
CUT 7
CUT 10
CUT 13
1½in
(4cm)
8in
(20cm)
1½in
(4cm)
5in
(12.5cm)
CUT 9
CUT 14
CUT 15
CUT 8
3in
(7.5cm)
1½in
(4cm)
FRONT

SIDE VIEW

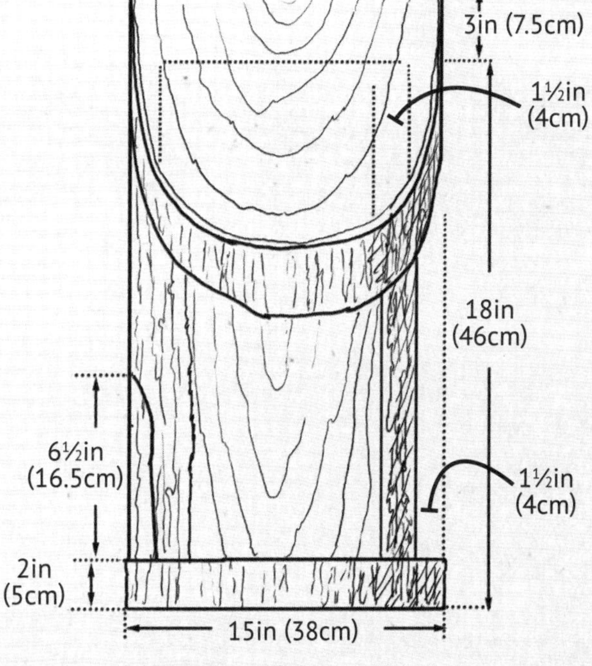

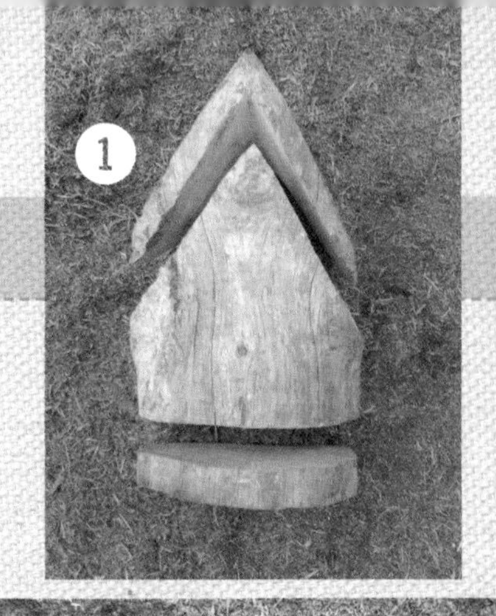

CUTTING AND JOINING

1 Find a deadwood log 15in (38cm) in diameter and 24in (61cm) long. Following the front cutting guide, mark cut lines #1–6 and make the cuts in that order. This creates three sections: roof, midsection and floor.

2 Follow the top cutting guide to mark cut lines #7–10 and #13–15 on the midsection. Using a 12in (300mm) blade on your reciprocating saw, make cuts #13–15.

3 Using a 16in (40cm) chainsaw, make cuts #7–10 by plunging through the wood with the chainsaw end and then following the cut lines in either direction to a stopping point. Once all the cuts have been made, you can remove the core in one piece.

4 Sand and wax the exposed wood on the hollow midsection (page 22).

5 Mark out cut #11, using the dimensions on the front cutting guide. Use a paddle bit to get a starter hole going, then switch to a 6in (150mm) reciprocating saw blade and follow the circumference you have marked to create the 3in (7.5cm) entrance hole. Sand around the edges.

Tip: When cleaning out a birdhouse, stick to the winter season in your region, when it's least likely to disturb any nesting rituals.

6 Using the back cutting guide, mark cut line #12, then make the cut. This creates the arched fairy door clean-out. In order to create a recessed doorway, you will need to cut the removed piece in half (see door detail sketch).

7 Thoroughly glue and reattach the midsection to the floor section, using 2in (50mm) nails in a crisscross fashion (page 21).

WHAT SIZE BIRD?

The 3in (75mm) entrance of this birdhouse will suit several species of small owls, including barred and boreal in North America, little in the UK and Tengman's (shown here) in Continental Europe.

Tip: Don't worry if an owl does not use the house straight away. Owls can take up to two years before they deem a house to be safe for them to inhabit.

FINISHING

8 Find a stick that is ¾in (2cm) in diameter and 4in (10cm) long. Cut it in half to create two 2in (5cm) sections. Place them on the floor inside the doorway, protruding slightly to create a permanent doorstop on the inside of the clean-out door. Fix them in place with glue and nails.

---

9 Using a ⅜in (9mm) bit, drill two peg holes, one on either side of the outside of the doorway entrance. Insert two small sticks into the peg holes to act as removable doorstops.

---

10 Glue and reattach the roof. Apply glue to the top of the roof and the bottom of the house so that all end grain is saturated. Set the house on its back and leave to dry overnight.

---

11 Using a ¼in (6mm) bit, drill a drain hole in the centre of the floor.

---

12 Decorate according to your own taste or use our house for inspiration.

Two sticks glued and nailed inside the clean-out doorway act as a permanent doorstop so that the door cannot accidentally be pushed inside the birdhouse.

Two small decorative sticks inserted into drilled peg holes in the floor hold the clean-out door in place on the outside.

Tree Stand

Our Tree Stand makes a great centrepiece for any garden, and can hold any flat-bottomed birdhouse in this book. This is an unusual project because it can be made from green fallen wood or chainsaw-cut wood. The sap in the wood can actually be a good thing in this case because sap makes it unappealing to insects of all kinds. This will prolong the life of your Tree Stand.

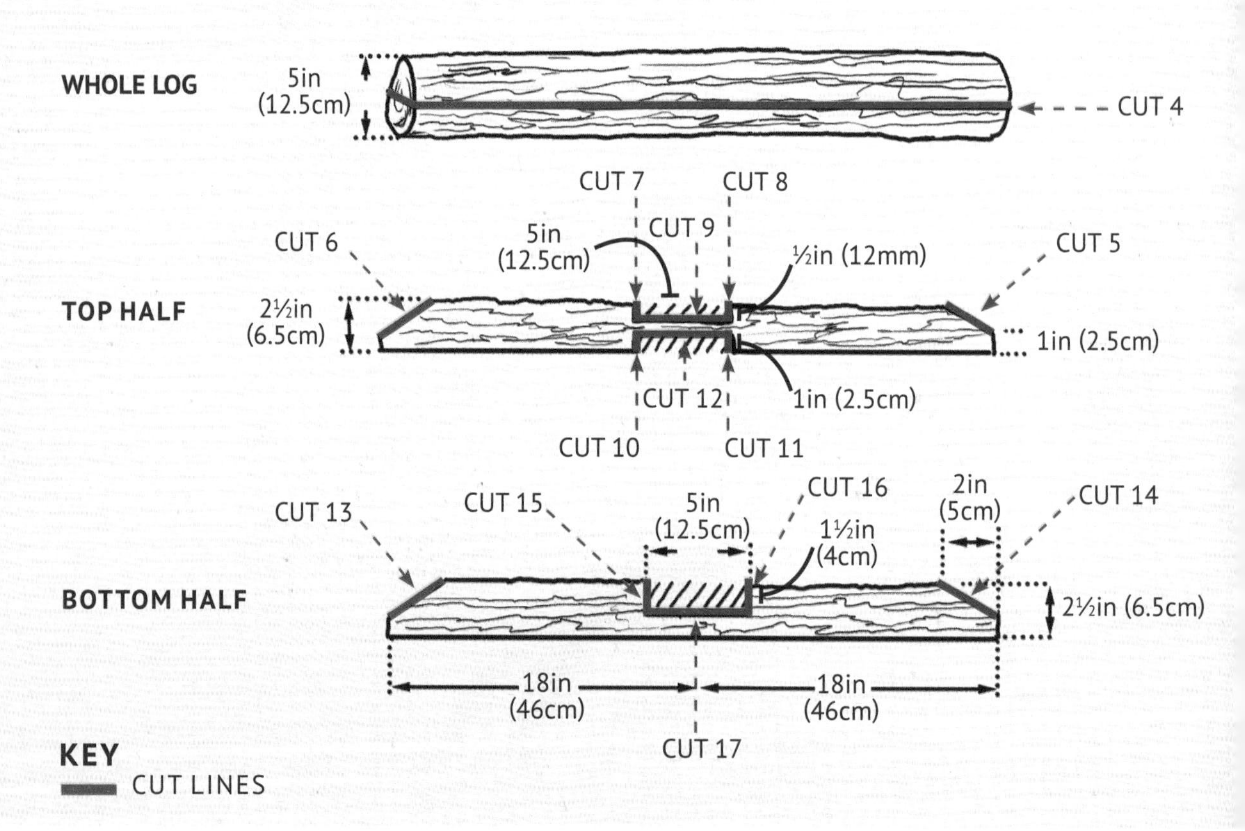

FRONT VIEW

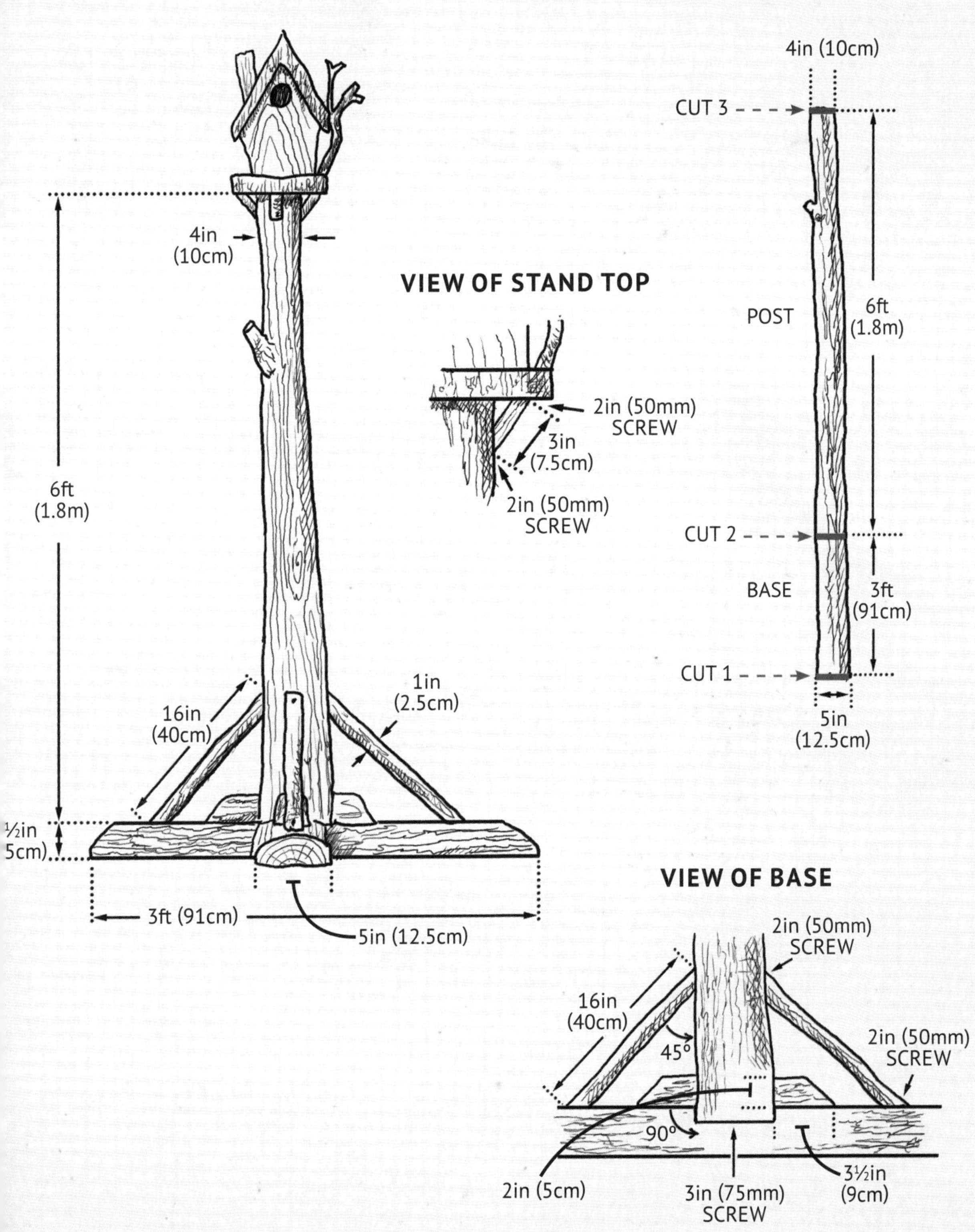
4in
(10cm)
6ft
(1.8m)
16in
(40cm)
1in
(2.5cm)
½in
5cm)
3ft (91cm)
5in (12.5cm)
VIEW OF STAND TOP
2in (50mm)
SCREW
3in
(7.5cm)
2in (50mm)
SCREW
CUTTING GUIDE: POST
4in (10cm)
CUT 3
POST
6ft
(1.8m)
CUT 2
BASE
3ft
(91cm)
CUT 1
5in
(12.5cm)
VIEW OF BASE
2in (50mm)
SCREW
16in
(40cm)
45°
2in (50mm)
SCREW
90°
2in (5cm)
3in (75mm)
SCREW
3½in
(9cm)

CUTTING THE LOG

1 Find a piece of downed tree about 10ft (3m) long. It should start at about 5in (12.5cm) in diameter and taper to about 4in (10cm). Square off the bottom using a framing square, with the centre line of the log as your baseline. This is cut #1. Measure up exactly 3ft (91cm) and make cut #2. Cut #2 is the most important one to be plumb and square because it forms the bottom of the Tree Stand's post.

---

2 On the long section of tree, measure up 6ft (1.8m) from where you just cut, and make cut #3, also perfectly square. Now you have created two sections with all ends perfectly square: the 3ft (91cm) section will become the base; the 6ft (1.8m) section will be the post.

---

3 Refer to the base cutting guide to mark and then make cut #4. This creates the top and bottom sections of the base.

---

4 Continuing with the base cutting guide, mark and make cuts #5 and #6. Then mark and make cuts #7–9, creating a ½in (12mm) deep notch in the centre of the uppermost side of the top piece. On the same piece of wood, mark and make cuts #10–12 to create a 1in (2.5cm) deep notch on the underside of the top piece. Set this piece aside.

---

5 Mark and make cuts #13–17 to create a 1½in (4cm) deep notch on the uppermost side of the bottom piece.

6 On a level working surface, put together the two 3ft (91cm) pieces to make a plus sign. If they do not fit just right, take the difference out of the notch made in the bottom section only. You can use a wood rasp, sandpaper or chisel. Do not remove any more wood from the top piece. Once they fit snugly, set both aside.

---

7 Find four strong sticks, 1in (2.5cm) in diameter and roughly 22in (56cm) long. Cut each stick to 16in (40cm) long with 45-degree angles on either end to form the struts for the base (see the base view and front view). This will leave four cut-off pieces about 4in (10cm) long. Cut each one to 3in (7.5cm) long with 45-degree angles on either end to form supports for the birdhouse on top (see the stand top view and front view). Set these pieces aside, keeping the 16in (40cm) branch pieces handy.

The short pieces are used to support the birdhouse on top.

The long pieces form the struts between the post and the base.

---

8 Now find a stick that is 2in (5cm) in diameter and about 24in (61cm) long to cut into the anchor pieces for the base (refer to the base view and front view). First cut one side flat by taking a slice off. Then cut the stick into four identical anchor pieces, each 3½in (9cm) long with a 90-degree cut on one end and a 45-degree cut on the other.

These anchor pieces hold the post firmly to the centre of the base.

Gather together and organise all the pieces, making sure that you have everything ready before beginning assembly.

9 Put the base together first, by laying the top piece over the bottom piece. Then stand the post upright into the notch you made in the top of the base. Apply glue to all the end grain. Securely attach the anchor pieces (made in Step 8) with 3in (75mm) deck screws around the base. Two screws per anchor will suffice.

Check the post for plumb fit as you attach the anchor pieces.

10 Next attach the 16in (40cm) branch pieces as shown in the base view, with two 2in (50mm) deck screws per branch.

11 Lay the whole stand on its side and put one 3in (75mm) deck screw through the middle of the stand. Make sure it anchors into the post. Glue the top of the post and the bottom of the stand to saturate the end grain, letting it remain on its side until thoroughly dried.

12 The last four pieces made in Step 7 are for when you are ready to attach the birdhouse to the top. First, pre-drill the holes for the screws with a ⅛in (3mm) bit. Centre the birdhouse of your choice on the top of the post. Attach each piece snugly to the post and the bottom of the birdhouse with two 2in (50mm) deck screws.

All holes for screws should be pre-drilled with a ⅛in (3mm) bit, at least 1in (2.5cm) deep.

The lip where the birdhouse meets the post forms a baffle, protecting birds from climbing predators.

Jungle Gym Feeding Station

This is a great variation of our Tree Stand. It provides endless entertainment and is built to last. You can use all our feeder designs in this feeding station, including the Nurse Log Planter (page 116) with a blooming flower for your bees and pollinators. The Wishing Well Seed Feeder (page 94) looks good on top.

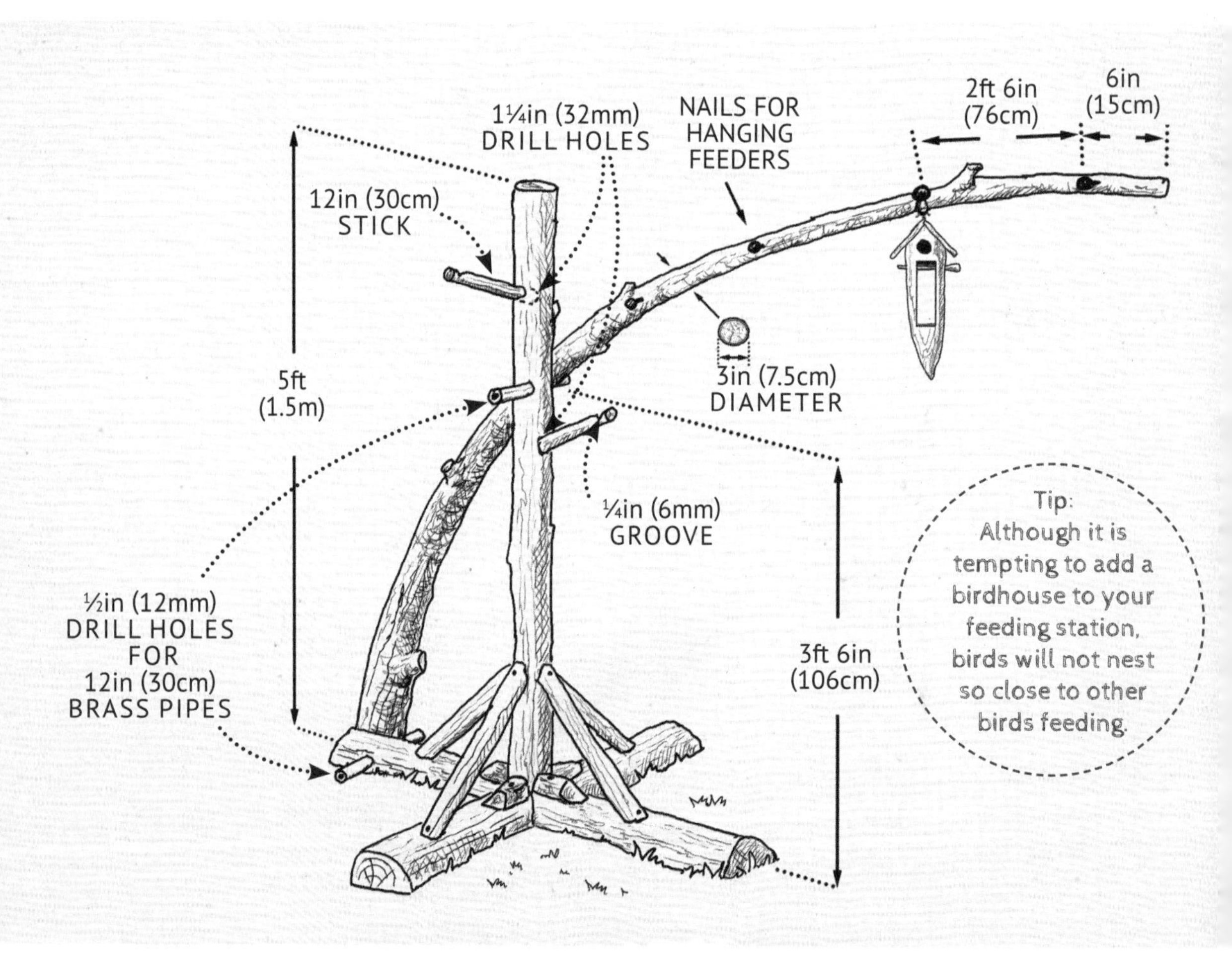

MAKING THE STAND

1 Begin by building the Tree Stand (page 86), but make it only 5ft (1.5m) tall instead of 6ft (1.8m). It must still be perfectly square on top. Look for a branch, roughly 3in (7.5cm) in diameter and 12ft (3.7m) long, with a natural curve in it. It can be drifted or forest-found. Referring to the sketch, line up the curved branch against the Tree Stand, and clamp the branch to the post and base of the stand.

2 Using a ½in (12mm) bit that is 12in (30cm) long, drill through both the post and the branch in one motion. Go in and out multiple times. Taking care not to move the branch, drill a hole through both the branch and the base in the same way.

---

3 Cut a ½in (12mm) brass pipe or hardwood stick into two 6–12in (15–30cm) lengths, and insert one in each drilled hole. Drill the holes again if the pipe or stick is too tight to fit.

4 Using a 1¼in (32mm) bit, drill two holes in the post of the Tree Stand to insert sticks for hanging feeders (see sketch). Each hole should be 2½in (6.5cm) deep and at a slight downward angle. Whittle a stick to fit snugly inside each one and protrude 8–12in (20–30cm). Using a wood rasp, make a little groove near the end of each stick to act as a catch for holding the feeders.

---

5 Find four ring nails about 2in (5cm) long, ⅛in (3mm) diameter, with a ⅜in (9mm) head, and attach them to the curved branch, starting about 6in (15cm) from the tip of the branch and spacing the nails about 2ft 6in (76cm) apart. Let them protrude ½in (12mm) to hang your feeders on. Use three 2in (50mm) deck screws to attach a feeder on top of the stand.

Wishing Well Seed Feeder

This is one of the most fun ways to feed wild birds. The small ones sit inside and feel comfortable, knowing they have protection from predators above. The bigger birds comically sit on the side and dip their heads in for another bite. It can hang anywhere, or can be mounted on our Tree Stand (page 86) or a fence post.

CUTTING GUIDE

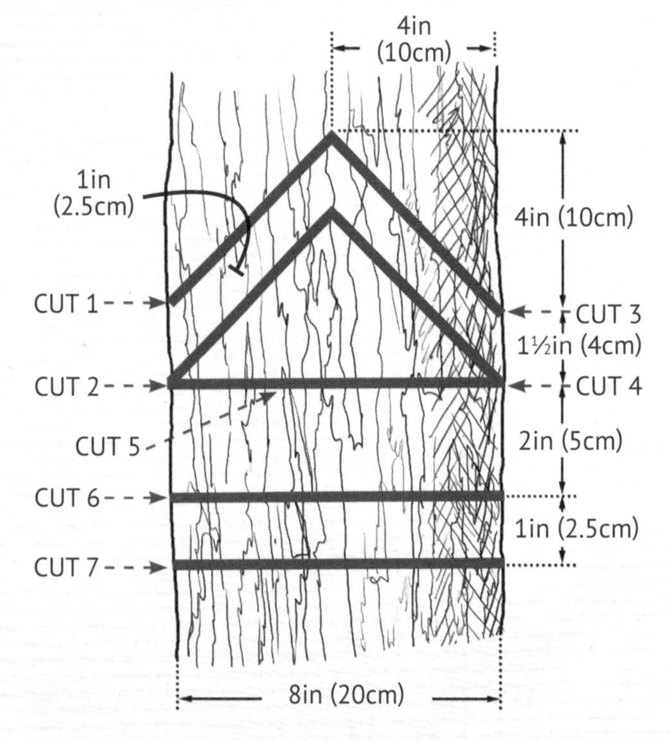

FRONT VIEW

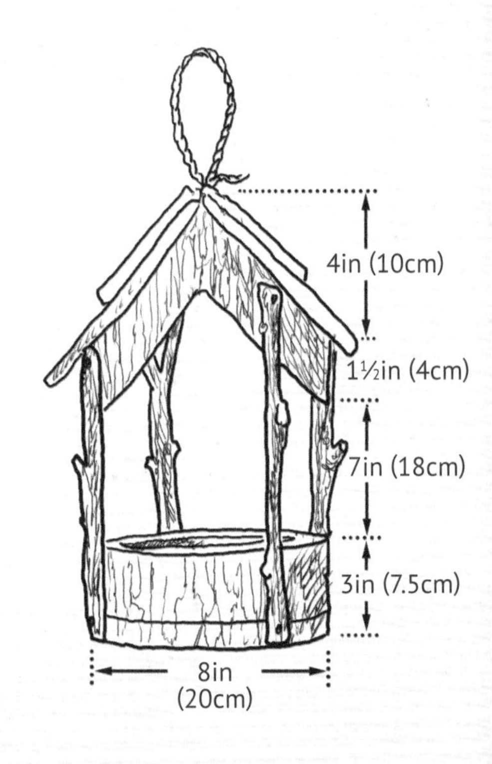

KEY

CUT LINES

CUTTING AND JOINING

1 Find a log about 8in (20cm) in diameter and 12in (30cm) long. Refer to the cutting guide and mark cut lines #1–7. Make cuts #1–7, creating three sections: the roof, bowl and floor. Glue the inside of the roof and set aside to dry while you work on the bottom.

2 Strap down the 'bowl' slice and hollow it out using the technique from the Flat-topped Birdhouse (page 34), until you have a ring of wood about 1in (2.5cm) thick.

3 Attach the bowl to the floor, using glue on both pieces and 2in (50mm) finish nails in a crisscross pattern (page 21).

4 Gather four sticks that are ¾–1in (2–2.5cm) thick and 14in (36cm) long. Lay the roof and the floor piece on a flat surface, aligning them, and attach two sticks at the ten and two o'clock positions, using 2in (50mm) finish nails in a crisscross pattern (see front view sketch).

5 Flip the whole thing over and attach the remaining two sticks to the other side in the same manner. Use secateurs to cut the sticks so that they are flush to the roofline and to the floorline.

It looks best when you follow the rings of the log when hollowing out the bowl of the feeder.

Snip the sticks flush and then stand up the feeder at this point to make sure it sits flat.

FINISHING

6 Use a ¼in (6mm) drill bit to put a drain hole in the centre of the floor piece. Then use the same bit to drill holes for the wire as seen in the wiring diagram.

7 Wire through with twisted PVC-coated wire and form a releasable loop on top (page 23). Thoroughly coat the end grain with glue and hang to dry overnight.

8 Use your imagination to decorate the feeder. We think of various different-sized birds and where they would land, and how they would move around the feeder. It's fun to see them alight on stick perches and manoeuvre closer to check a spruce cone for seeds inside, in between mouthfuls of seeds from the bowl.

WIRING DIAGRAM

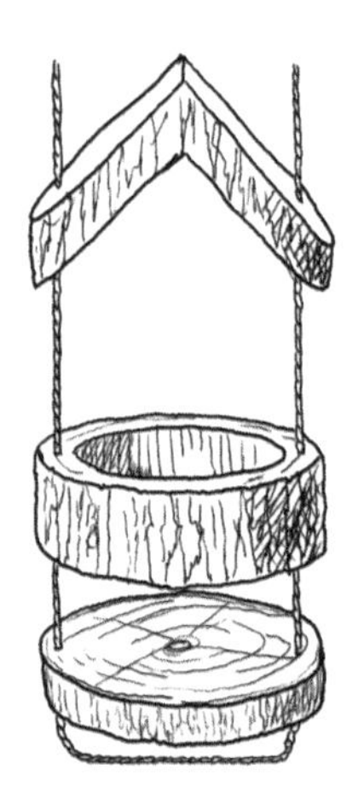

Tip: You do not have to use sapless birdhouse wood to make this feeder, but it does need to be wood that has cured properly so that it does not split over time.

Peanut Butter Feeder

This is the favourite feeder in our garden. We fill it twice daily with chunky peanut butter and every bird from chickadees to downy woodpeckers want a bite. We also put one where the Douglas squirrels can access it. Everybody loves a peanut!

FRONT VIEW

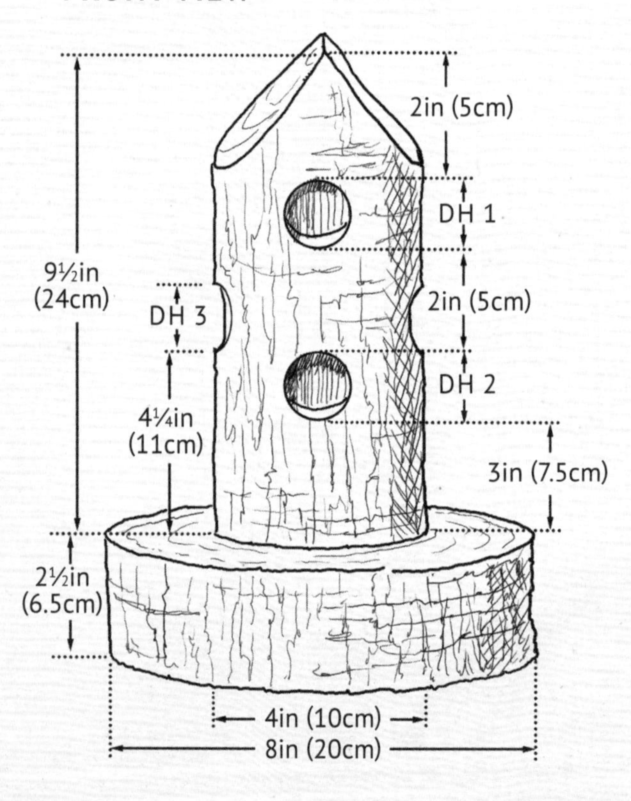

CUTTING GUIDE: BACK

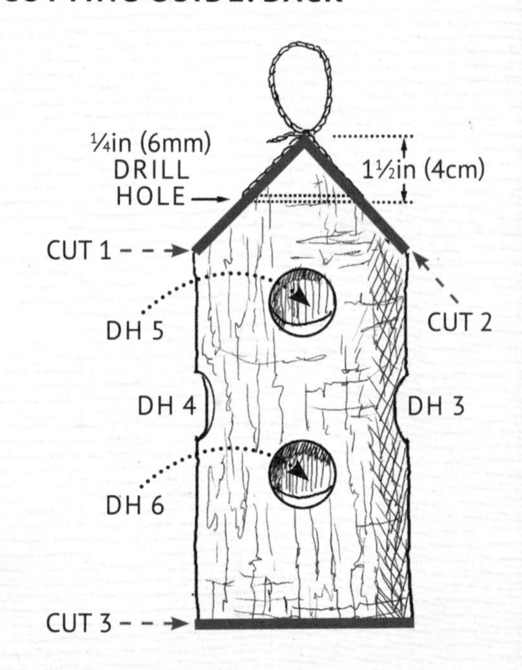

KEY

CUT LINES

DH 1–6 = 1¼in (32mm) DRILL HOLES

MAKING THE FEEDER

1 Look for a piece of good birdhouse wood that is 4in (10cm) in diameter and 12in (30cm) long. It is important to use sapless wood because sap trapped inside wood fibres will create mould over time with the daily application of peanut butter. You also need a slice 8in (20cm) in diameter and 2in (5cm) thick to provide a base for the birds to sit on while eating.

2 Mark the cut lines according to the cutting guide. Make cuts #1–3. Using a 1¼in (32mm) bit, drill holes #1–6, referring to both sketches. Each hole should be about ¾in (2cm) deep.

3 Glue the bottom of the house to the middle of the top of the base slice, then attach with 2in (50mm) nails in a crisscross fashion (page 21).

4 Using a ¼in (6mm) bit, drill a hole straight across the roof area. Wire through according to the cutting guide and form a releasable loop on top (page 23). Now glue the rest of the exposed end grain: the sides of the roof and both sides of the 8in (20cm) base. Hang to dry overnight.

5 When decorating a feeder like this, think about where birds will sit to access the peanut butter circles. If you see a certain species having trouble getting a grip, or reaching, you can add pieces to make it easier for them. Feel free to add pieces here and there for the birds waiting for their turn, too. Sometimes parents bring their babies to the feeder; the baby birds wait on a stick just a few inches away while the parent accesses the peanut butter and feeds it to them.

Fairy Door Suet Feeder

This suet feeder is one of the most popular items in our catalogue. It has a narrow, arched doorway on each side, only big enough for fairies to pass through, and for birds to eat through. Birds unequivocally love to stand on the feeder and eat their suet through the little fairy doors.

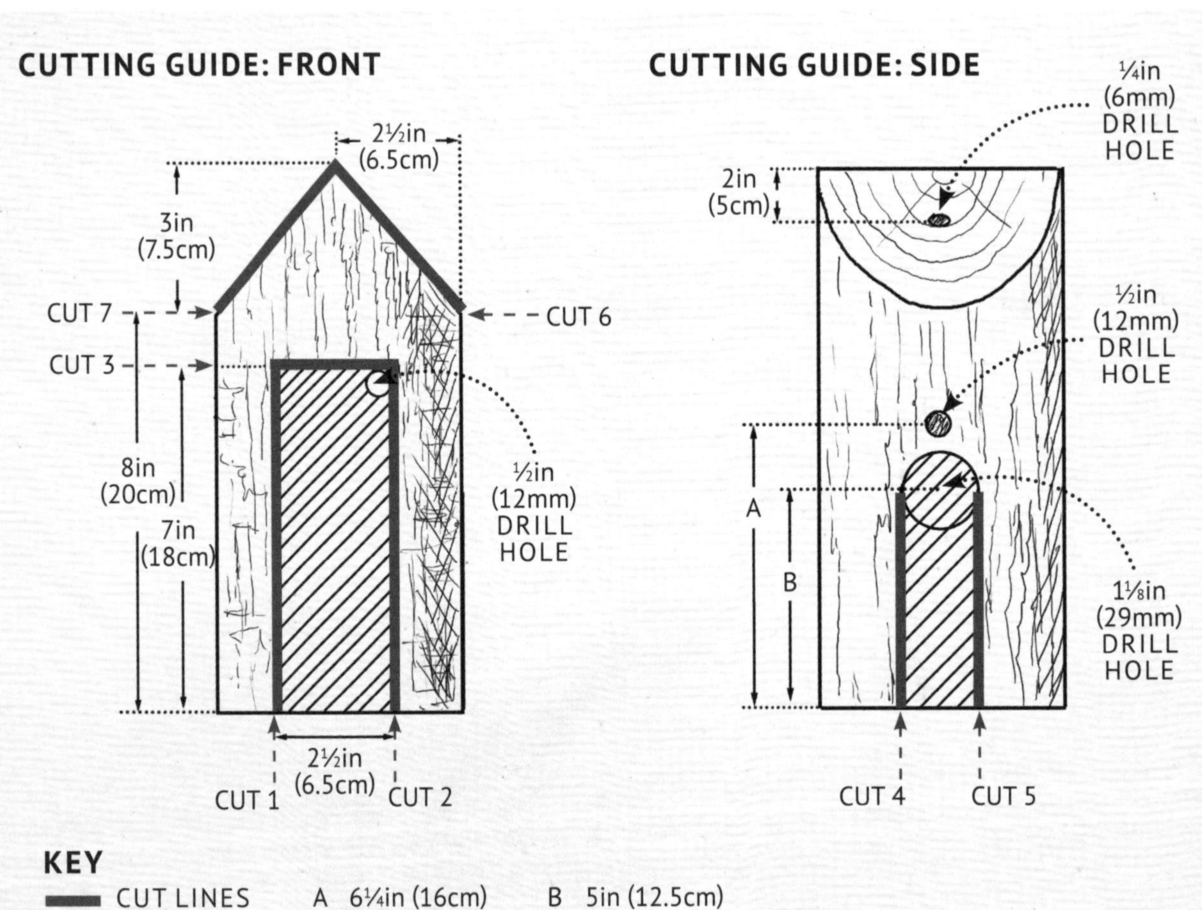

MAKING THE FEEDER

1 Find a deadwood log 5in (12.5cm) in diameter and 12in (30cm) long. Mark according to the cutting guides. Using a ½in (12mm) bit, drill a starter hole in the top corner of the front doorway (see front cutting guide), then use a reciprocating saw with a 6in (150mm) blade to make cuts #1–3. Set aside the centre piece to use as the base.

2 Referring to the side cutting guide, rotate the log 90 degrees and measure 6¼in (16cm) up from the bottom. Make a mark in the centre and drill straight through, using a ½in (12mm) bit that is 6in (15cm) long. This will be where you will insert a stick to hold the suet cage in place.

3 Measure 5in (12.5cm) up from the bottom and make a mark right in the centre. Using a 1⅛in (29mm) paddle bit, drill straight through the log to create the arch at the top of the fairy doors. Switch back to the 6in (150mm) saw blade and make cuts #4 and #5 to finish the doors.

4 Make cuts #6 and #7, creating the roof peak. With glue and nails, attach the centre piece that you set aside in Step 1 to the bottom of the feeder, creating a 'floor' for the birds to stand on.

5 Find a stick that is ½in (12mm) or less in diameter and at least 7in (18cm) long. Whittle it to taper one end. This will hold the suet cage in place.

6 Using a ¼in (6mm) bit, drill a hole straight across the roof, 2in (5cm) down from the peak. Thread twisted wire through and form a releasable loop on top (page 23). Coat all the end grain with glue and hang the feeder to dry overnight. Place a suet cage inside the feeder, using the whittled stick to suspend it. Decorate to your liking.

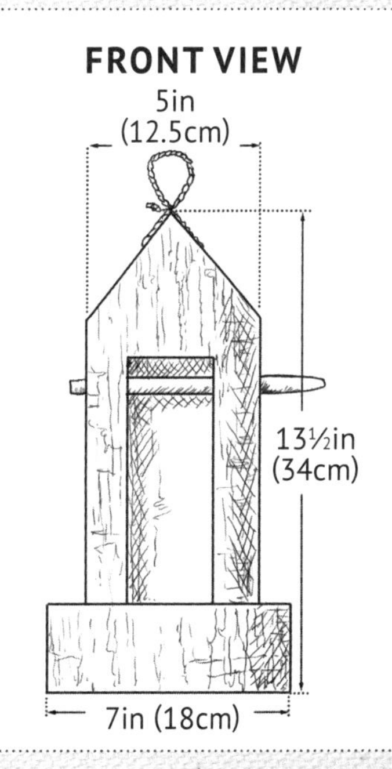

End-piece Suet Feeder

This is a great feeder for bird watching. You can find the wood for it along edges of rivers or on a beach. Woodpeckers can enjoy this feeder by fanning their tails on it, and small flocking birds sometimes cover it in turns. We add holes for chunky peanut butter, so that this feeder has two treats for wild birds.

CUTTING GUIDE

CUT 5
CUT 6
DH 3 FRONT
DH 4 BACK
DH 1
CUT 1
DH 7
CUT 2
CUT 4
DH 6
DH 2
CUT 3
DH 5

KEY
CUT LINES
DH 1–7 = DRILL HOLES

FRONT VIEW

5½in (14cm)
2¼in (5.5cm)
6½in (16.5cm)
4in (10cm)
2½in (6.5cm)

SIDE VIEW

4in (10cm)
½in (12mm)
6½in (16.5cm)
2½in (6.5cm)

MAKING THE FEEDER

1 Find a piece of drifted deadwood that starts about 5½in (14cm) in diameter and runs a length of no less than 10in (25cm) before tapering off for a few inches. Mark your log according to the sketches and then strap it down, above the top of the drawn peak. This is the widest part of the wood and a good place to hold it for the majority of the work.

2 Using a ½in (12mm) bit that is 12in (30cm) long, make drill holes #1 and #2 through the entire width of the wood (see the cutting guide). Using a 6in (150mm) blade on a reciprocating saw, plunge through the holes and make cuts #1–4. The centre falls out when the cuts are connected.

3 Using the same bit, make drill hole #7 through the entire piece. This creates the entrance hole for the whittled stick. Make drill holes #5 and #6, using a 1¼in (32mm) paddle bit and going all the way through the wood. With the same paddle bit, make drill holes #3 and #4, but only go ¾in (2cm) deep. These holes are perfect for peanut butter.

4 Make cuts #5 and #6, creating the roofline and removing the structure from the portion strapped down. Using a ¼in (6mm) bit, drill a hole straight across the roof, 2¼in (5.5cm) down from the peak. Thread twisted wire through and form a releasable loop on top (page 23). Glue all the exposed end grain and hang to dry overnight.

5 Find a hardwood stick ¾in (2cm) in diameter and 8in (20cm) long. Whittle it into the shape shown in the sketch. This becomes the pin that will hold the suet cage in place. Decorate to your liking, adding a roof for weather protection and perches for eating.

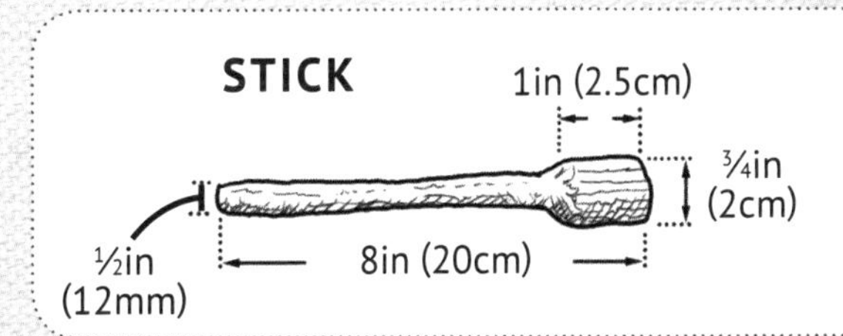

Pollinator Houses

This project makes three different houses in varying heights. There are places for ladybirds to lay eggs between the barked roof and the body of the house. Some butterflies also use the undersides of the bark to lay their eggs. Mason bees will fill the chambers with pollen and eggs, alternately. Pollinating moths sometimes use the chambers as protection while knitting their cocoons.

MAKING THE HOUSES

1 Find a piece of good birdhouse wood about 3–5in (7–12.5cm) in diameter and 20in (51cm) long. Referring to the cutting guide, mark the log with cut lines for all three houses. Make cuts #1–8 in that order, working your way up the log. This will result in three birdhouse-shaped pieces.

2 Using a ¼in (6mm) bit, begin to drill the chamber holes into the medium-sized house (see the medium house front view). The first hole should be 1½in (4cm) down from the peak. Drill through the log, almost to the other side. (Using a drill bit shorter than the log diameter makes it easy not to drill all the way through.) Drill the second hole 1½in (4cm) down from the first, and then a third hole 1½in (4cm) down from that.

CUTTING GUIDE

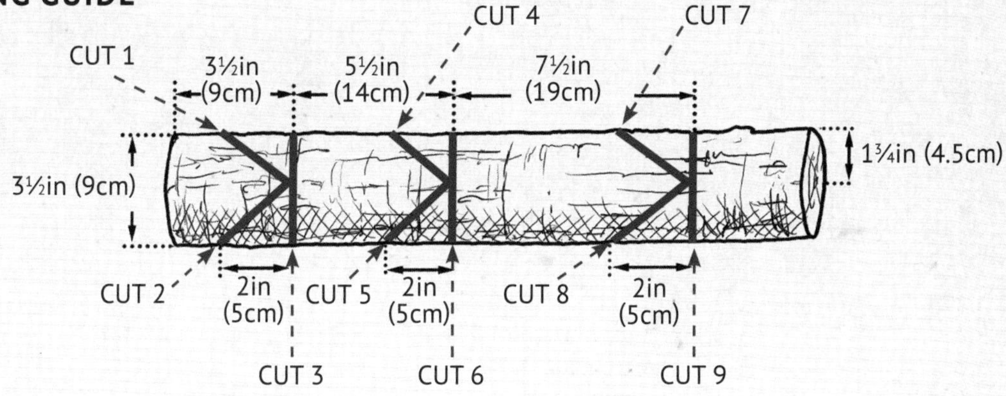

FRONT VIEW OF SMALL HOUSE

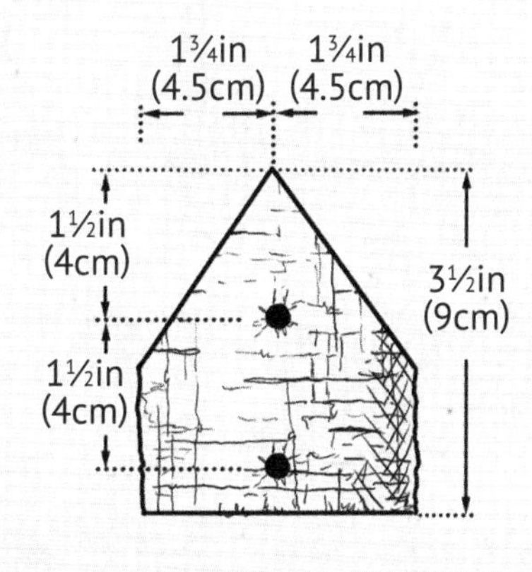

FRONT VIEW OF MEDIUM HOUSE

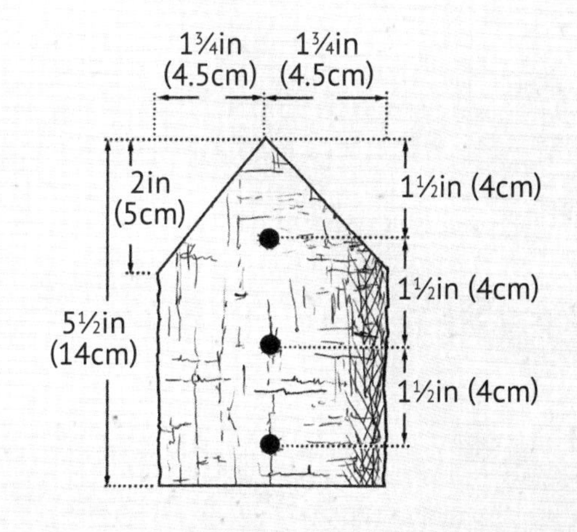

FRONT VIEW OF LARGE HOUSE

1¾in (4.5cm) 1¾in (4.5cm)

1½in (4cm)

1½in (4cm)

1½in (4cm)

1½in (4cm)

7½in (19cm)

TOP VIEW OF EACH HOUSE

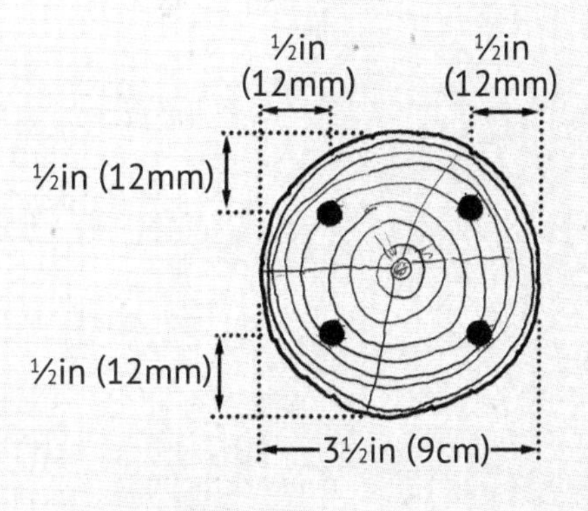

KEY

CUT LINES

● ¼in (6mm) DRILL HOLES

3 Turn over the medium piece, and this time measure down 2in (5cm) from the peak and drill the first chamber on the reverse side of the house. Measure another 2in (5cm) down for the next one.

4 Now drill the chambers in the large and small houses using the same principle. On one side, start drilling 1½in (4cm) down from the peak and drill at 1½in (4cm) intervals until you run out of room. On the other side of both, start 2in (5cm) down from the peak for the first chamber. Note that on the small house, this is the only hole you will have room to make on the reverse side.

5 On the bottom of each house, drill four ¼in (6mm) holes, spaced evenly (see the top view).

6 Using the ¼in (6mm) bit, drill a wire hole across the top of each house. String through a single strand of PVC-coated tie wire and form a releasable loop on top (page 23).

7 Coat the top and bottom surfaces of each house with glue and hang to dry overnight.

8 Decorate all three houses to your liking. You can match elements of each to create a village feel, or you can treat each house as an individual art object. You may like to give the houses to loved ones so that you all have a piece from the very same log.

WHAT SIZE BEE?

There are 129 different kinds of mason bees in North America alone. They range in size from tiny to quite large. We have used a ¼in (6mm) drill bit for the chambers in this example, but you can choose varying widths or a size that you know corresponds to your local bees' needs.

Tip: If you wish, you can use a woodburner to darken the holes to make them stand out more.

Bumblebee House

Bumblebees look for exactly the same qualities in their homes as the rest of the wild kingdom. They need the dry, sap-free, temperature-controlled environment of our deadwood log. It acts like a Thermos, but in this case keeps the wet conditions and extreme hot or cold at bay. For more information on where to mount and site your pollinator house, see page 27.

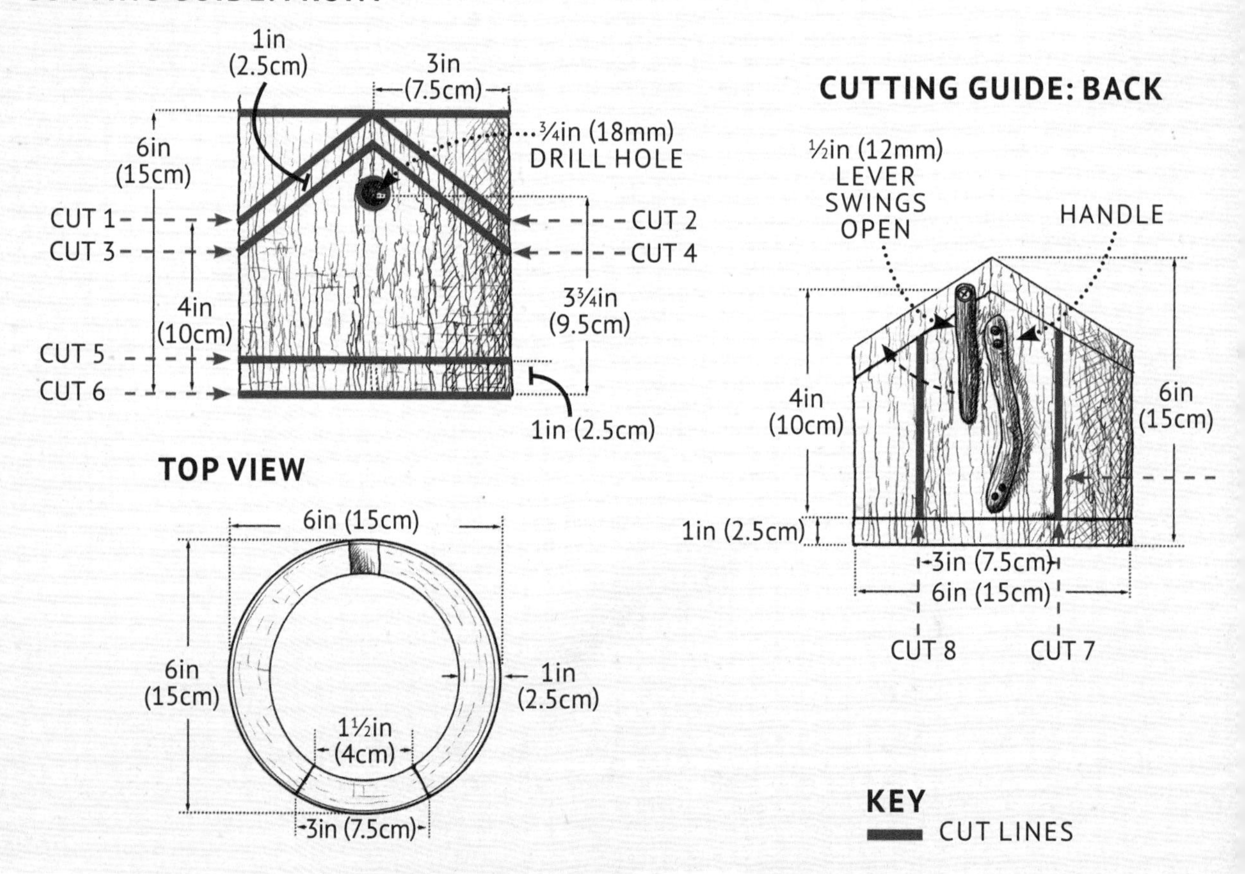

CUTTING AND JOINING

1 Look for a log 6in (15cm) in diameter and 8in (20cm) long. Use the front cutting guide to mark cut lines #1–5. With a reciprocating saw and a 9in (230mm) blade, make cuts #1–5 in that order. Mark and then drill the entrance hole with a ¾in (18mm) drill bit.

2 Set aside the roof and floor pieces and strap down the midsection for hollowing. If the wood you have found is relatively soft, hollow out as for Project 2 (page 40). If the wood is hard, follow the steps for Project 1 (page 34). Once your midsection is hollow, with about ¾in (2cm) thickness of wood around the outside, mark and then make cuts #7 and #8 (see the back cutting guide). This creates the door.

---

3 Attach the midsection to the floor of the house using glue on both sides and 2in (50mm) finish nails in a crisscross fashion (page 21). Do not attach the door.

4 Attach the roof with glue and crisscrossing 2in (50mm) finish nails, being careful not to push down too hard. The door piece needs to be able to slide in and out as required. Apply glue to the end grain all the way around the little door, and let all pieces dry thoroughly before moving on. Once dry, apply wax and tung oil mixture (page 22) over the dried glue all around the door so that the glue can never reconstitute and dry the door into place.

DOOR DETAIL

4in (10cm)

3in (7.5cm)

APPLY WAX

½in (12mm) GAP

3½in (9cm)

FINISHING

5 See top view and door detail sketches for assembling the removable door. You will need two hardwood sticks, both about ½in (12mm) in diameter. One should have a curve in it and be 3½in (9cm) long for the handle. The other should be straight and 3in (7.5cm) long for the lever. Attach the curved stick to the door with 1in (25mm) finish nails: two in the top, none in the curve and two in the bottom. Put the door into place on the house. Position the straight stick next to the handle and, holding it in place, use a ⅛in (3mm) bit to drill into the stick and roof section, penetrating ½in (12mm). Use a 2in (50mm) ring nail or screw to hold the stick in place, creating a simple lever system.

The lever swings outwards for easy removal of the door.

---

6 Using a ¼in (6mm) bit, drill a wire hole across the top of the house. String with a length of twisted PVC-coated tie wire and form a releasable loop on top (page 23). Coat the top and bottom of the house thoroughly with glue and hang to dry overnight.

---

7 Decorate the house in any way you like (the bee will not use the materials like a bird). When you have finished decorating, open the back door and fill with various fluff. Bumblebees use the same nesting fluff as wild songbirds. This includes your family pet's hair, cat-tail fluff, goat and sheep hair and milk thistle fluff.

The bee does not use the outside of the house at all, the way a bird family uses it, so the decoration is just for fun and your own viewing pleasure.

Fluff Dispenser

Our Fluff Dispenser is a practical and whimsical way to help birds find what they need for nesting, in a place where you can witness the magic. You get to interact with the birds by putting your own brush hair or the hair from family pets into the dispenser, then watch the birds take the hair back to their nest. You can also supply them with plant-based fluff, such as cat-tail fluff and mosses.

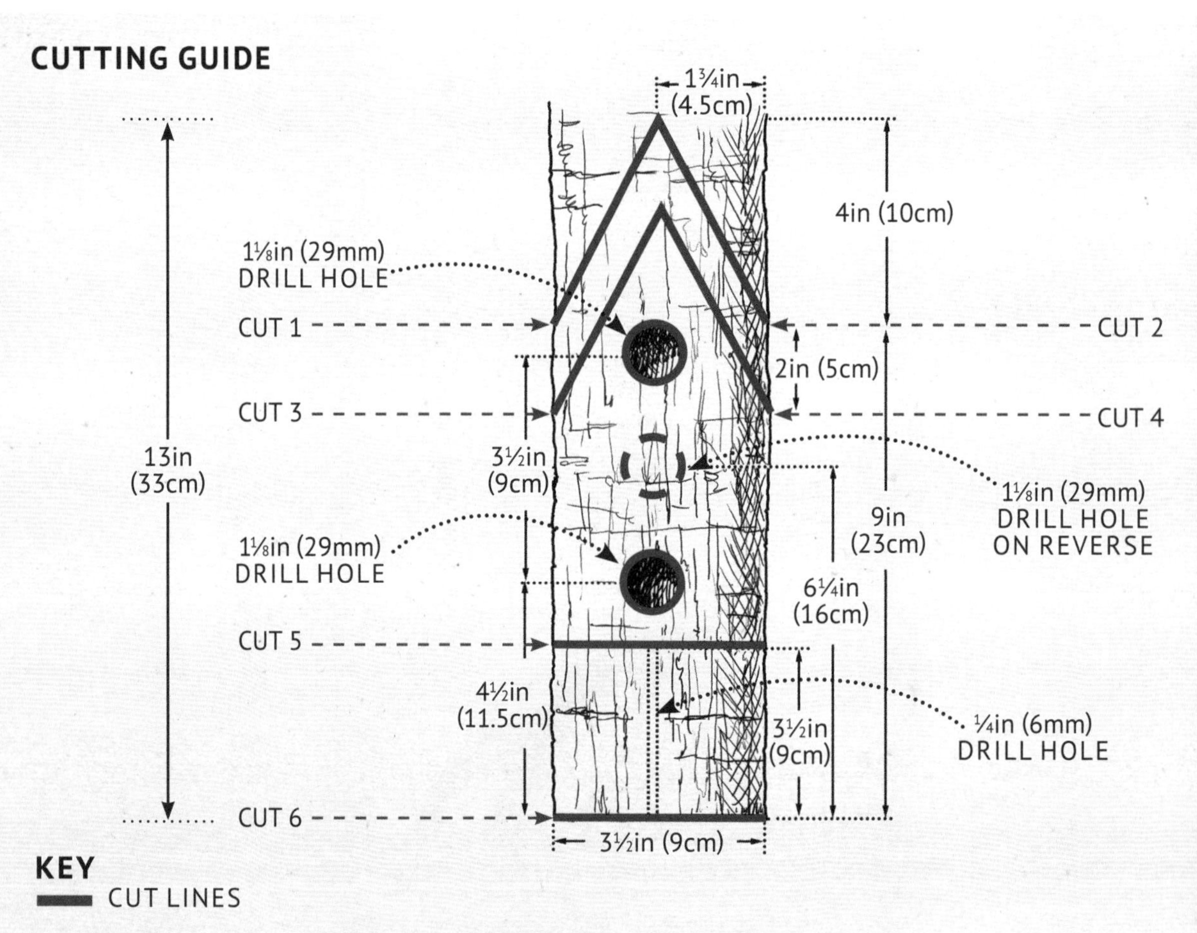

CUTTING AND JOINING

1 Find a piece of good birdhouse wood 3in (7.5cm) in diameter by 14in (36cm) long. Referring to the cutting guide, mark and make cuts #1 and 2, creating the roofline. Then mark cut lines #3–6.

2 Using a 1⅛in (29mm) paddle bit, drill the two holes on the front of the midsection. Make the first hole ½in (12mm) above the floorline and go about 1in (2.5cm) deep. Drill the second hole near the roof peak, also about 1in (2.5cm) deep. Now turn over the piece and drill another hole in the middle of the back of the midsection. This ensures that none of the three holes you have made intersects.

Use a wood rasp and then 80-grit sandpaper to smooth out the cavity. A rough interior will catch and hold the fluff pieces. You want the birds to access it freely.

3 Make cuts #3–6, creating three sections: roof, midsection and floor. Hollow out the midsection following the steps in Project 1 (page 34) until you are left with a ring of wood about ½in (12mm) thick. Smooth the cavity with a wood rasp and sandpaper.

4 Glue and then nail the midsection to the floor piece using 2in (50mm) finish nails in a crisscross pattern (page 21). Apply glue to the inside of the roof and the end grain of the roof peak on the midsection piece. Keeping them separate, leave them to dry.

5 Attach shingles to the roof for both decoration and rain protection (page 24), using 1in (25mm) finish nails in a crisscross pattern. Attach different perches that the birds might use while getting the fluff from the holes, using 2in (50mm) finish nails and only nailing them to the floor piece. If you put a perch near the top hole, attach with 1in (25mm) nails to avoid penetrating the smooth cavity.

FINISHING

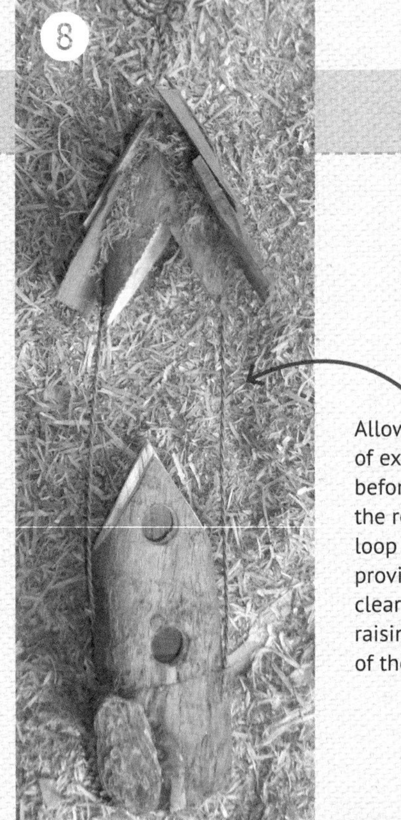

Allow 6in (15cm) of extra wire before forming the releasable loop on top to provide enough clearance for raising the roof of the dispenser.

6 Using a ¼in (6mm) auger bit, drill holes for the wire to go through. The wire will go up through the bottom piece, then out the sides and travel outside the dispenser before going up through the roof shingles on either side.

7 Make a drain hole with the same auger bit. It is important that if water gets inside during a windy rainstorm, it can drain out instead of remaining inside the fluff dispenser.

8 Make a 4ft (1.2m) length of twisted PVC-coated wire and insert the ends up through the holes made in Step 6. Form a releasable loop at the top (page 23), but instead of making the loop directly above the roof, for this project you need to position the loop a full 6in (15cm) above the peak so that the roof can be raised for filling the dispenser.

9 Look for two small sticks that will act as guides for sliding the roof down into place after filling the dispenser. They should be as tall as the body of the dispenser, but not prevent the roof from coming all the way down. Attach the sticks with 1in (25mm) finish nails, but do not shoot any nails into the roof. The roof needs to move freely. Then coat the bottom of the fluff dispenser with glue and hang to dry overnight.

Fill the dispenser with fluff and hang it where you can see your birds use it.

Note: Dryer lint is ONLY good for wild birds if you do not use any kind of fabric softener or dryer sheets. The chemicals in those items stay in the lint and cause problems for birds.

Nurse Log Planter

This planter is the ultimate in fertile forest science. It uses the properties of deadwood to nurture new life, just as happens in the wild. These planters provide natural warmth and water retention, which all root systems appreciate. This is also a good use of wood that is too soft to be used for birdhouses.

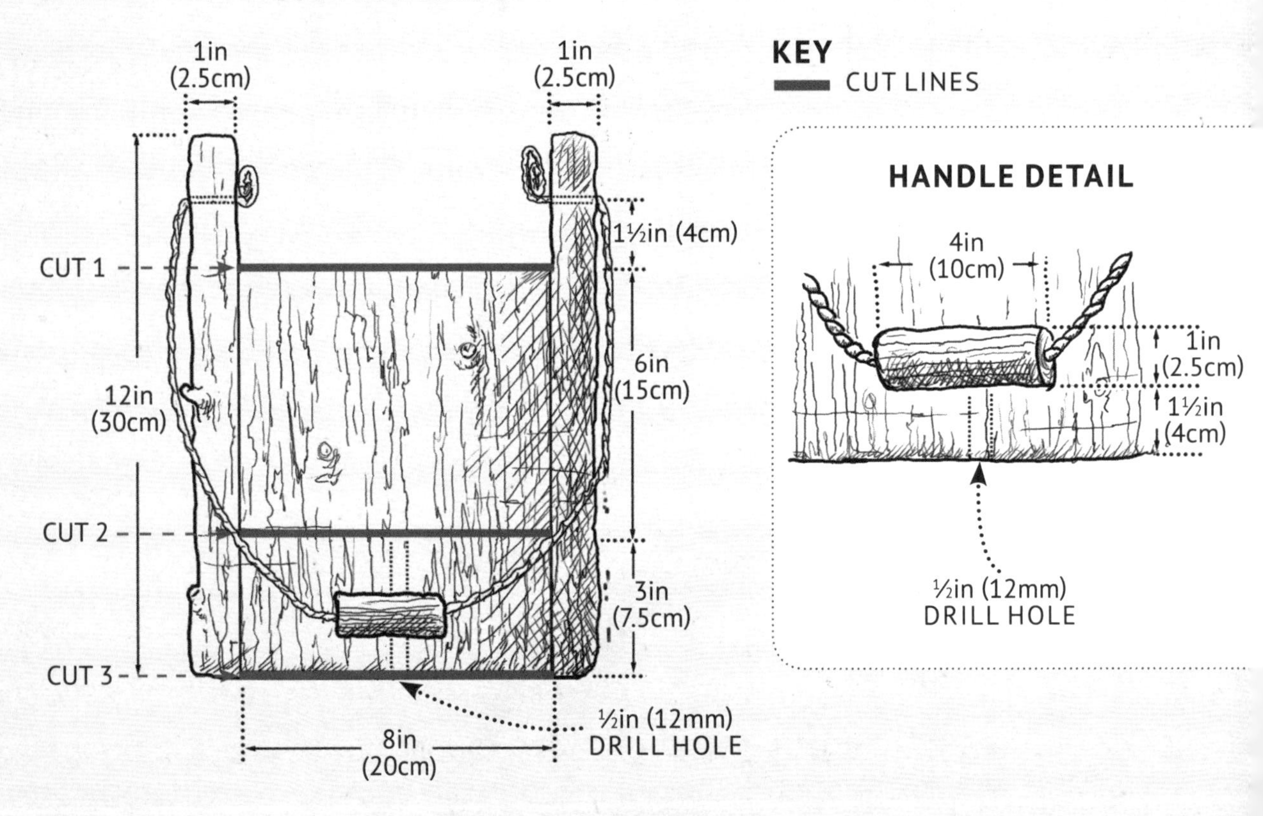

CUTTING AND JOINING

1 Find a deadwood log 6–12in (15–30cm) in diameter. Here we are using an 8in (20cm) log. Strap it down securely. Using a reciprocating saw with a 12in (300mm) blade, cut the end of the log to give you a flat surface (cut #1 on the cutting guide), then make a directional mark on the end grain.

2 Measure down 6in (15cm), make cut #2 and set the piece aside. This will form the bowl of the planter.

3 Make a directional mark on the log in the same way as before. Measure down 3in (7.5cm) and make cut #3. This piece will form the bottom of the planter.

4 Strap down the 6in (15cm) section and hollow it out. If the wood you have found is relatively soft, hollow out as for Project 2 (page 40). If the wood is hard, follow the steps for Project 1 (page 34). Continue until there is 1½in (4cm) of solid wood left around the outside.

Using the growth rings as guidelines when hollowing out the log makes for a more attractive planter.

5 Apply glue to the top of the bottom piece and to the bottom of the hollowed piece and join them together firmly with 2in (50mm) nails in a crisscross pattern (page 21). Using a ½in (12mm) bit, drill a drain hole in the centre of the bottom piece.

FINISHING

6 Find two sticks that are approximately 1–1½in (2.5–4cm) in diameter and 12in (30cm) long. Attach one stick to either side of the log vertically with 2in (50mm) nails. Measure 1½in (4cm) up from the top of the planter and make a mark on both sticks. Using a ¼in (6mm) bit, drill through each stick horizontally.

---

7 Find a stick that is 1½in (4cm) in diameter and 4in (10cm) long. Drill a ¼in (6mm) hole lengthways through its centre. This creates the handle.

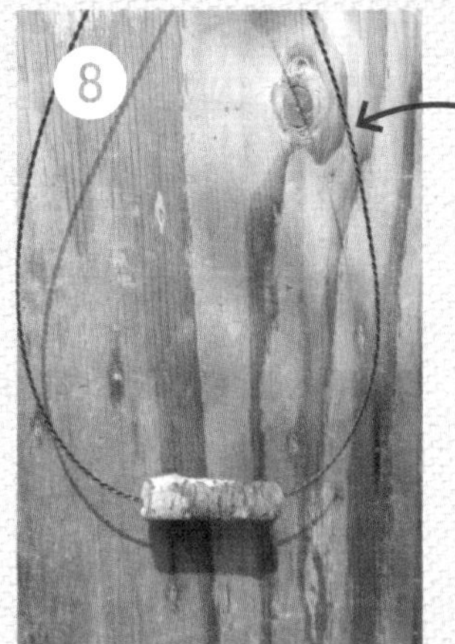

Don't use PVC-coated wire for the handle. Bare metal wire will look more in keeping with the natural rustic planter.

8 Make a 20–30in (50–75cm) length of twisted tie wire (page 23). Thread the wire through the handle, leaving the handle in the centre. Curve the wire into a half moon and thread it through the holes in the side sticks, towards each other in the centre. Using needle-nose pliers, twist both ends into a spiral until you get a good handle length remaining. Bend each spiral flush against the stick.

9 Glue the top and bottom end grain of the log planter and rub in some sawdust to fill any gaps that may be present. Lay the planter on its side and allow to dry overnight. Add decorative elements around the outside and then you are ready to plant.

The bare metal wire handle will weather and deteriorate slowly and naturally with the planter.

Single Chamber Bat House

Bats need the exact same conditions that birds are looking for in the wild. Their houses need to be warm and dry and free of any sap that would turn to mould over time. Bats tend to be extremely sensitive, and the properties of deadwood support their immune system in a way that milled timber cannot.

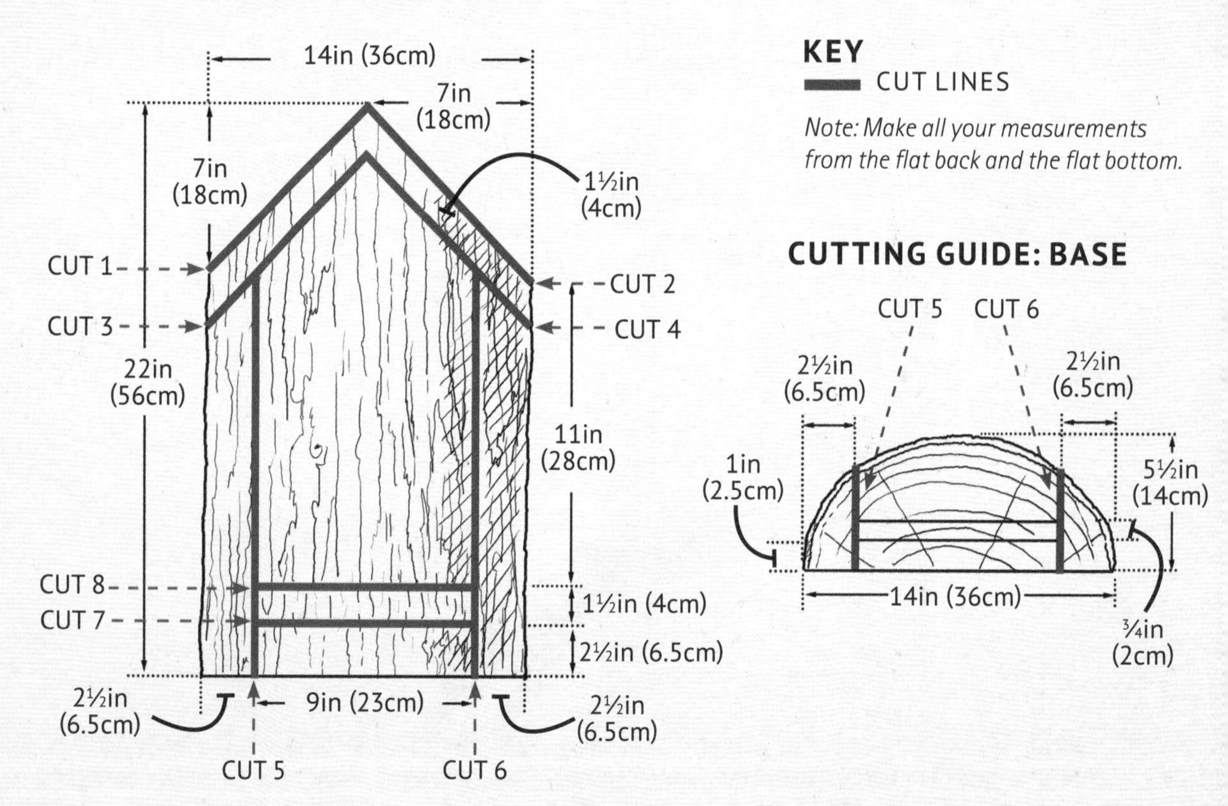

CUTTING THE LOG

1 Find a good piece of birdhouse wood that is a half log. You want a semicircular shape about 14in (36cm) wide, 5½in (14cm) deep in the middle and 22in (56cm) long. The photos and sketches will help you visualise this. Mark your log according to the front cutting guide.

2 Make cuts #1–4 in that order, creating a peaked roof. Set it aside. Referring to the front and base cutting guides, make cuts #5–6 and remove both side pieces. Set them aside for reattachment later.

3 Referring to all cutting guides, mark the main piece all the way around. Then make cut #7 to a depth of 4½in (11.5cm) and then cut #8 to a depth of 2in (5cm). Make cut #9 and remove the front face of the log. You may discard this piece or save it for later use.

4 Sand the remaining piece and then apply a wax and tung oil mixture (page 22) to seal and protect the exposed woodgrain. The wax protects it from glue when you reassemble the pieces.

5 Now make the ¾in (2cm) rough groove that will serve as the bat's actual house. Use a chainsaw to excavate the wood marked for removal (cut #10). Stop the cut 2in (5cm) below the peak.

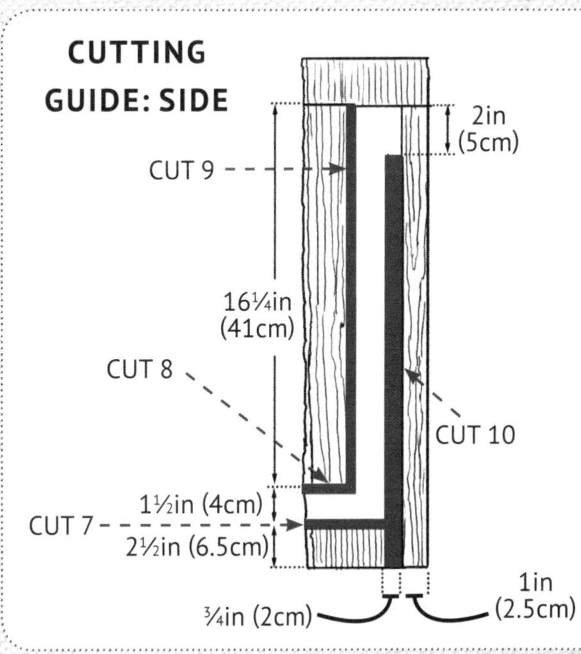

JOINING AND FINISHING

6 Reattach both side pieces by saturating them with glue and using 2in (50mm) finish nails in a crisscross fashion (page 21).

7 Glue and attach the roof in the same manner, being careful not to shoot nails that will penetrate the house's hollow cavity. Rub sawdust in the seams to seal them and fill any gaps.

8 Turn the bat house on its back to create the hanging system. Measure 15in (38cm) up and 4in (10cm) in from both sides and make a mark for a nail. Hammer a 2in (50mm) nail into each mark at a 45-degree angle upwards and outwards. Make a short length of twisted PVC-coated wire (page 23) and wind it around the nails to form a hanging loop.

9 Coat the top and bottom of all end grain thoroughly with glue and then hang the bat house to dry overnight.

10 Decorate to your liking. Bear in mind that these houses hang far up, so your decor should be bold and have high contrast in order to enjoy it at such a distance.

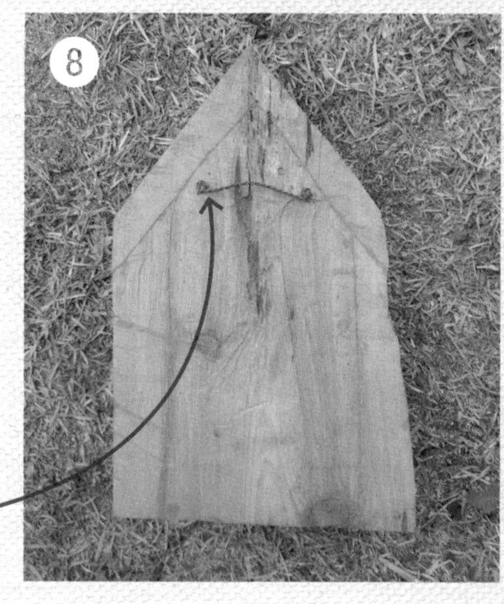

If the bat house is allowed to hang perpendicular to the ground, any babies inside would fall out. With this hanging system, the bat house hangs at an angle so that the babies can stay inside until they are ready to fledge.

Double Chamber Bat House

This house is made of dry and sapless redwood, a great choice for bats because the dark colour provides extra warmth for their delicate constitutions. Always mount your bat habitat on a south-facing post, tree or exterior wall to let the wood soak up all the day's sunshine and warmth.

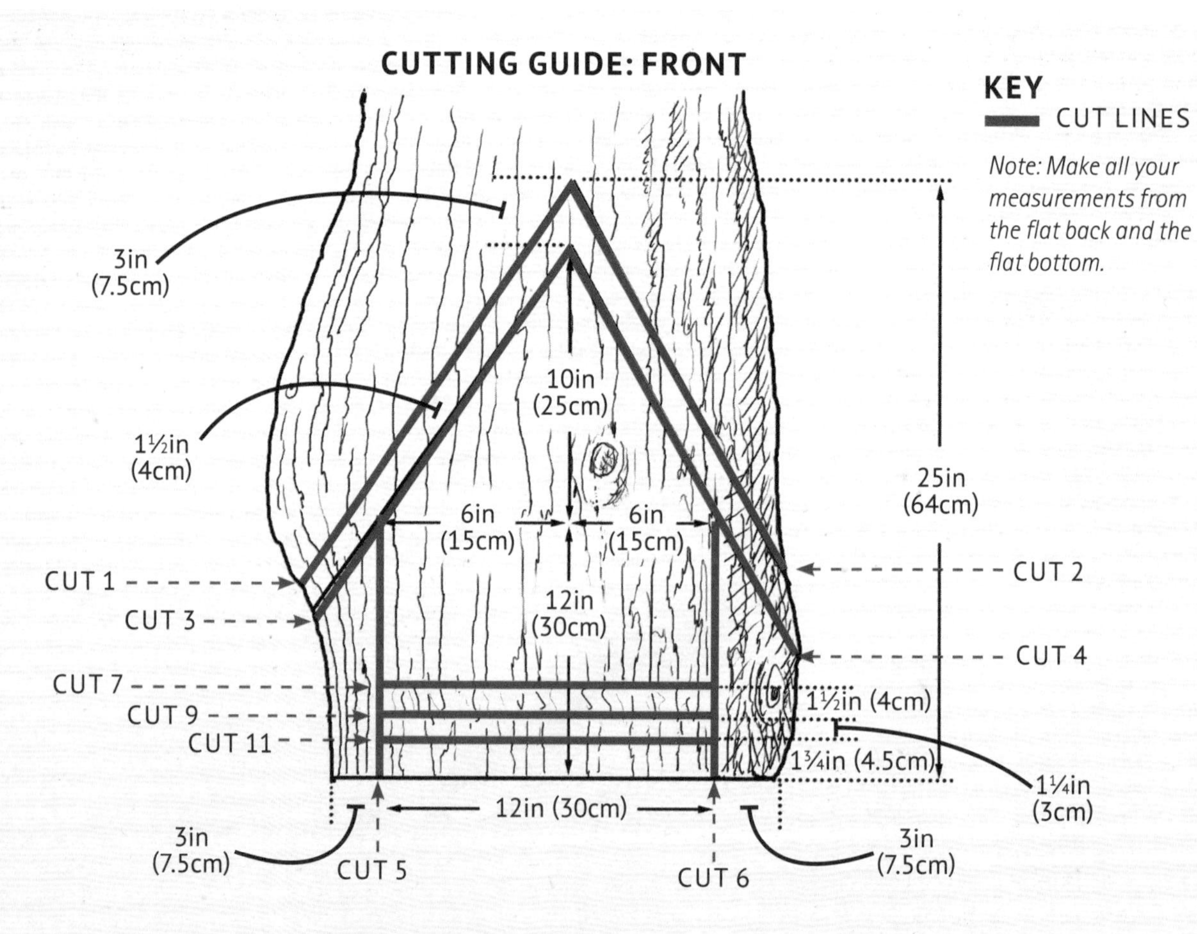

MAKING THE HOUSE

1 Find a good piece of deadwood that is half of a big log: 18in (46cm) in diameter, 28in (71cm) long and 8in (20cm) deep at the round of the arc (see the base cutting guide). Strap down the log and mark according to the front cutting guide.

2 Using a 12in (300mm) reciprocating saw blade, make cuts #1–6, in that order, to remove the roof and side pieces. Set them aside for later.

3 Using all the cutting guides, mark cut lines #7–12 on three sides. Make cut #7 to a depth of 3in (7.5cm) and then cut #8 to a depth of 17½in (44cm). Removing this piece creates the face of the bat house. Sand the face and apply a wax and tung oil mixture to seal (page 22).

Sand and buff the exposed front face to seal the wood.

Shading in all the portions of wood to be removed makes the design much easier to understand at a glance when you have your chainsaw running.

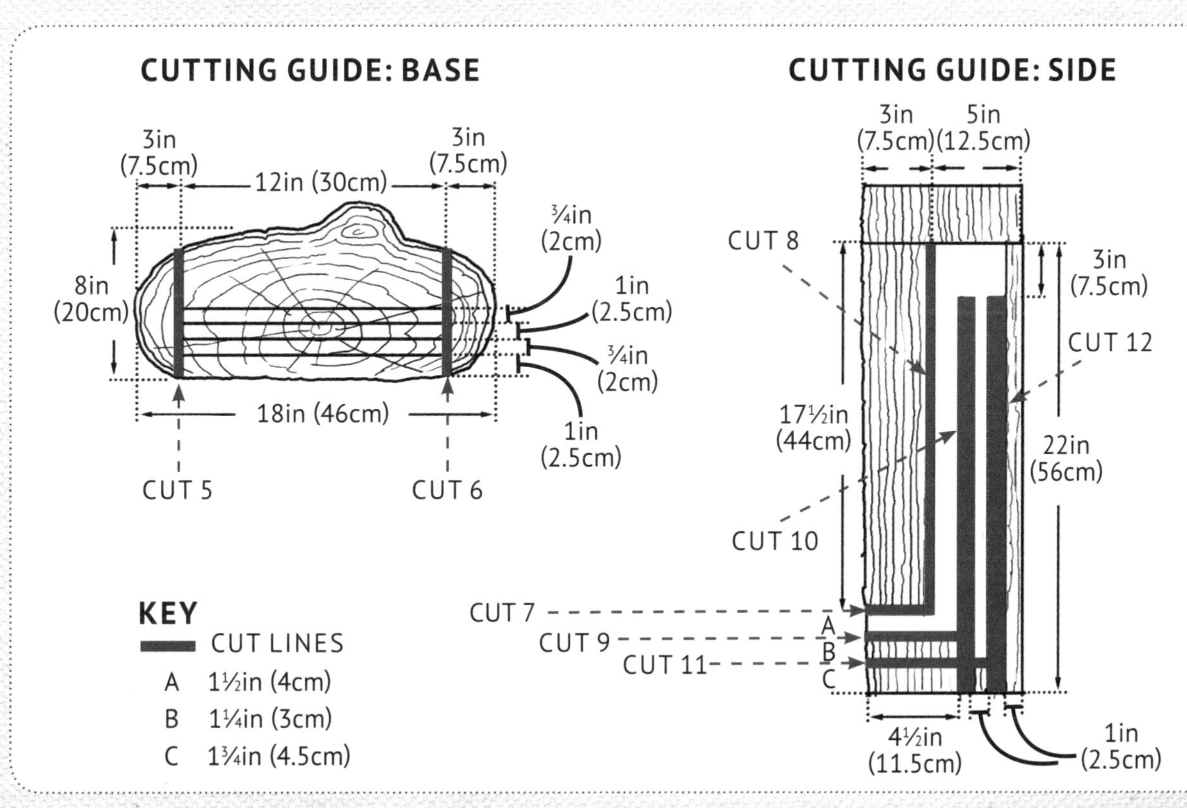

4 Make cut #9 to a depth of 4½in (11.5cm) and then stop. Switching to a chainsaw, make cut #10, passing through it a few times until it opens up to ¾in (2cm). This creates one of the grooves that serve as the bat's house.

5 Switch back to the reciprocating saw to make cut #11 to a depth of 1in (2.5cm). For cut #12, switch back to the chainsaw and follow the procedure used for cut #10 to create a second ¾in (2cm) groove.

6 Reattach the right and left sides using glue and 2in (50mm) finish nails in a crisscross fashion (page 21). Then reattach the roof in the same manner.

7 Add a twisted wire hanging loop on the back as for the Single Chamber Bat House (page 23). Thoroughly coat the top and bottom of all end grain with glue and hang to dry overnight.

8 Decorate the house with any natural elements you want. You can make it look homely and hobbity or modern and abstract, depending on the choices you make. Bear in mind that bat houses usually hang far up in the air so they need dramatic decor to show at that distance. High contrast looks great; think of using light silver driftwood sticks, for example, on a redwood bat house.

This house is perfect for attracting a new colony of bats. Bats build colonies over time. It begins with one or a few that seek out and find the perfect conditions. Then they will gather friends and nest together until they make a thriving community. They cuddle as close together as possible, all day.

WHAT SIZE BAT?

This and the previous bat house project are suitable for microbats of all kinds, depending on your area.

Bats ideally want to live 16-20ft (5-6m) up, so mount your bat chamber up high.

A QUANTUM BOOK
First published in the UK in 2015 by
Apple Press
74–77 White Lion Street
London N1 9PF
United Kingdom

www.apple-press.com

ISBN 978-1-84543-580-6

QUMNTBH

This book was designed and conceived by
Quantum Books Ltd
The Old Brewery
6 Blundell Street
London N7 9BH

Production manager: Rohana Yusof
Publisher: Kerry Enzor
Design: David Rose, Lucy Parissi
Editorial: Cary Hull, Michelle Pickering, Donna Gregory
Photography of the birdhouses: Curt Peters of Digital Dunes Photography
Step-by-step photography: Amen and Maria Fisher
Sketches for the birdhouses provided by Amen Fisher, additional work by Andrew Pinder

Printed in China by 1010 Printing International

10 9 8 7 6 5 4 3 2 1

Acknowledgements

Quantum Publishing would like to thank the following for supplying images for inclusion in this book:

Page 4 shutterstock/Paul Reeves Photography, pages 11–12 shutterstock/Bryan Eastham, page 13 shutterstock/Vetapi (top); Paul Reeves (middle); StockPhotoAstur (bottom), page 13 shutterstock/ Bildagentur Zoonar GmbH (top); Gucio_55 (middle); Trofimov Denis (bottom), page 14 shutterstock/Karin Jaehne, page 15 shutterstock/geertweggen (top); Brian Dicks (bottom), page 16 shutterstock/geertweggen, page 28 shutterstock/MVPhoto (left); Menno Schaefer (center); Radka Palenikova (right), page 29 shutterstock/Stephen Farhall (left); Katarina Christenson (center); Trofimov Denis (right), page 33 shutterstock/MVPhoto, page 40 shutterstock/Alan Scheer, page 55 shutterstock/StevenRussellSmithPhotos, page 56 shutterstock/Toni Genes, page 60 shutterstock/Bildagentur Zoonar GmbH, page 64 shutterstock/Paul Reeves Photography, page 70 shutterstock/Mike Truchon, page 83 shutterstock/ Bildagentur Zoonar GmbH, page 106 shutterstock/Vetapi, page 126 shutterstock/Stephen Farhall

All other images are the copyright of Quantum Publishing. While every effort has been made to credit contributors, Quantum Publishing would like to apologise should there have been any omissions or errors and would be pleased to make the appropriate correction to future editions.

Thanks to Tim Harris for his help with the UK edition.